ONE

ONE

A Small Group Journey Toward
Life-Changing Community

Nick Cunningham
with Trevor Miller

Abingdon Press / Nashville

ONE
A Small Group Journey Toward Life-Changing Community
By Nick Cunningham with Trevor Miller
Copyright © 2016 by Abingdon Press
All rights reserved.

Scripture quotations in this publication, unless otherwise indicated, are from the Common English Bible, © Copyright 2011 by Common English Bible, and are used by permission.

Scripture quotations noted NRSV are taken from the New Revised Standard Version of the Bible, copyright 1989, Division of Christian Education of the National Council of the Churches of Christ in the United States of America. Used by permission. All rights reserved.

ISBN-13: 9781501816451

16 17 18 19 20 21 22 23 24 25—10 9 8 7 6 5 4 3 2 1

Manufactured in the United States of America

Contents

Introduction

In John Chapter 17, just before Jesus is arrested and eventually crucified, we find him praying. He begins by praying for himself, and then he prays for his disciples. But in verses 20-26, Jesus prays for . . . us. Jesus prays for you and me and everyone who believes in him because of the disciples' witness.

What Jesus prays for is quite remarkable. In verses 21 and 22, Jesus prays that we would be one, just as he and the Father are one, and in verse 23 Jesus prays that we would be brought to complete unity, made "perfectly one."

One.

Unity.

When we hear that word unity we tend to think of some sort intellectual agreement. To our ears, unity means we hold the same values and generally agree on what we think or believe. As a result, we regard unity as something we can have from a distance. This is not the sort of unity that Jesus has in mind, however. In his words, we are to become "perfectly one" (John 17:23). Jesus desires for our unity to reflect what he has with the Father—a complete oneness. This oneness will actually be a conduit through which we experience God's love.

This sort of unity, becoming perfectly one, isn't something we can have from a distance. It requires us to get up-close and personal with each other. This kind of unity is the result of a common experience and a shared life.

Notice what Jesus says will be the result of our unity. In verse 21, Jesus prays that all of us will be one just as he and the Father are one. Then he goes on to say, "I pray that they also will be in us, so that the world may believe that you sent me."

So that the world will believe that you sent me.

Wow.

As Jesus looks ahead, he sees one thing that will prove to the world that this kingdom of God movement isn't just another flash in the pan but that it's straight from the Creator. And that one thing is the unity of Jesus' followers.

Jesus knew that his followers were going to face challenges that would be too big for them to handle on their own. Jesus knew that they would need to make some serious changes in their lives that they couldn't make on their own. Most importantly, Jesus knew that his followers would be able to do more and be more together than they could ever do or be on their own. And so when Jesus prays on behalf of all of his followers—including you and me—Jesus prays for one thing: unity. He prays for us to have the same love, a shared life, so that we would be perfectly one.

If you are reading this, then you are somehow drawn to this sort of connection with other followers of Jesus. You get a sense of why it matters, and you want it for yourself. Wanting it and experiencing it, however, are two different things. What we have to understand is that this level of community doesn't happen by itself. It must be intentionally built and carefully sustained over time. This curriculum will help you get started, but it can only take you so far. It's up to you and the other members of your group to commit yourselves to one another over the long haul. It's up to you to develop and nurture your relationships with one another, moving towards the perfect oneness that Jesus envisions.

Our time together will be divided in two four-week sections. During the first four weeks, we will use the early church as our guide and explore the three Core Practices that go into forming Christ-centered community: pushing one another forward, lifting one another up, and sending one another out. We will also begin to embrace the three Core Postures that help us sustain life together: vulnerability, compassion, and grace. In these first four chapters, you will find some key teachings on each of these aspects of Christ-centered community. You should plan to read over this material in the first half of each chapter in advance. You will also find some opportunities for individual Scripture study and reflection during your group time together. There will be plenty of time in your group session to write or draw your thoughts about the Scriptures and the questions provided, so you don't need to complete these activities before you meet.

The second four weeks is all about putting what we have learned into practice. Through guided conversation, you and your group will develop a covenant statement based on the three Core Practices and create ground rules that reflect the three Core Postures. You will prepare to share and interact with one another's life stories to deepen your knowledge of your fellow group members. All of this will help ensure that you get started in the right direction and provide you with the tools you need to ensure that you stay headed that way. There is no teaching content to read in advance for these chapters, though you may find it useful to review the material from the first four weeks. You will find similar opportunities for individual creative reflection to guide your discussions during your group meeting. Again, this is designed to be used during your meeting, so you do not need to complete this in advance.

At the end of each chapter, you will find daily Scripture readings and brief questions to guide personal devotional time during the week. Using these will help you prepare for a thoughtful, open discussion during your weekly group meeting.

After the second four weeks, you will be on your own. The eighth week is not an end; it is a beginning. I pray that you will continue to live alongside one another in Christ-centered community, reflecting the oneness that God desires.

Session 1:

ONE LIFE

Have you ever noticed how your favorite memories are often connected to your favorite people?

For instance, during my junior year of college I had this unique opportunity to play American football in Italy with some of my closest friends. American football is a relatively new sport in Italy, and even though there is a lot of interest in the game there isn't a lot of knowledge or experience in terms of how it's played. So a team of former and current football players was assembled, and we hosted a camp for the Italians in the city of Rome. For about two weeks, I got to play a sport I love with some of my closest friends in one of the most incredible places on the planet . . . tough gig, right?

You know, when I think about that trip, which was one of my all time favorites, more than I remember the sites, or the culture, or the food I remember all of the great times that I had with some of my closest friends. Our favorite memories are almost always connected to our favorite people. At the same time, our most painful moments in life usually have something to do with a relational break. All of this is a reflection of how we are wired. We are wired for connection— for relationships.

We have been made in the image of a God who is best understood as Trinity: Father, Son, and Holy Spirit. God: three in one. The concept of God as Trinity is a difficult one to grasp, and I'm not sure we will ever really understand how it works. But we can be sure of what it means: God isn't just *in* a relationship; God *is* relationship. You and I have been made in the image of this relational God, which makes us deeply relational creatures. That means that our connection with one another isn't just something that we do. It is a vital part of who we are.

It shouldn't come as a surprise then what happens when the Holy Spirit explodes onto the scene at Pentecost. One of the first things that happens is this diverse group of people from all over the world, and from seemingly every walk of life, come together in the kind of community that we all long for, but so few of us ever experience.

Over the next few weeks, we are going to spend a lot of time with two passages in Acts: Acts 2:32-37 and 4:32-37. There is plenty to admire about how the early church lived with one another, but in his commentary *Acts for Everyone, Part One: Chapters 1–12* (Westminster John Knox Press, 2008), N. T. Wright points out that Luke, the author of Acts, is up to something in these passages that we cannot miss. Let's zero in on the description in Chapter 4, which Wright discusses on pages 73–78 of his book.

In just five short verses, the author of Acts references two Old Testament passages. The first one is in verse 32 when he says, "The community of believers was one in heart and mind." This is a reference to Jeremiah Chapter 32, where God is speaking about how the restored people of God will live once they are brought back from exile. In Jeremiah 32:39 God says, "I will give them one heart and one mind so that they may worship me all the days of their lives, for their own good and for the good of their children after them."

The second Old Testament reference is in Acts 4:34, when Luke tells us that as a result of God's grace, "there were no needy persons among them." This is a nod back to Deuteronomy Chapter 15. Deuteronomy was like the constitution for the nation of Israel. It was a description of how they were to live out their identity as the covenant people of God. Deuteronomy Chapter 15 speaks of a practice that was to take place every seven years where the people would forgive one another of any debt. "Every seventh year you must cancel all debts. This is how the cancellation is to be handled: Creditors will forgive the loans of their fellow Israelites. They won't demand repayment from their neighbors or their relatives because the LORD's year of debt cancellation has been announced" (Deuteronomy 15:1-2). Verses 4 and 5 go on to say, "Of course there won't be any poor persons among you because the LORD will bless you in the land that the LORD your God is giving you to possess as an inheritance, but only if you carefully obey the LORD your God's voice, by carefully doing every bit of this commandment that I'm giving you right now."

Here we begin to see what Luke, the author of Acts, is up to in Acts Chapter 4. He isn't just painting a beautiful picture of how the early church lived; he is also making a profound and even provocative statement about who these believers were. These people were the ones receiving the promised blessings of Deuteronomy and Jeremiah. This community of people who had centered themselves around the person and work of Jesus Christ wasn't just some sort of mob who knew how to throw a mean potluck supper. They were in fact the true covenant people of God—what God had been working toward all along and what the outpouring of the Holy Spirit had made possible.

Let's consider this for a moment. According to Luke, what marked the early church as the covenant people of God was a radical demonstration of community, which was grounded in their common commitment to Jesus. It wasn't their buildings that set them apart. It wasn't their rituals and traditions. It wasn't their higher morality or their family heritage. What identified this group as God's people was the remarkable unity that they lived out. This group of many, through the power of the Holy Spirit, had become one.

This shouldn't come as a surprise to us. In fact it makes perfect sense when we consider the larger biblical story. Sin separates us from God and from one another. Salvation draws us together, restoring our unity with God and with our fellow human beings.

We see from the very beginning that sin separates. In Genesis Chapter 3, the first human beings disobeyed God. Sin entered the picture, and as a result God's good creation was fractured. When the man and the woman realized they were naked, they were filled with shame and hid from their Creator (Genesis 3:8). Eventually, they were sent away from the garden of Eden, where they had enjoyed fellowship with God (3:22-24). The very first instance of sin manifested itself as division between humanity and God. When God questioned them about what happened, the man's first response was to blame the woman (Genesis 3:12). We see in that moment a rift between human beings. This division among human beings continues to escalate through the early chapters of Genesis: Cain kills his brother Abel, committing the first murder (Genesis 4), and the whole human population becomes scattered after God confuses everyone's language at the tower of Babel (Genesis 11). As the Book of Genesis unfolds, we see enmity between the sexes, outright violence among brothers, and the division of the whole earth into people groups who cannot even understand one another. Not only does sin separate us from God, it separates us from one another.

Now for the "good news." Where sin is about division, the gospel is about unity. In both Ephesians and Colossians, the apostle Paul refers to what God is doing through Jesus as a cosmic reconciliation. To reconcile means to bring back together or to rejoin. So through Jesus, God is bringing back together that which has been fractured: our relationship with God and with one another.

Essentially, this is what we witness at the start of the Book of Acts. In Acts 2, we read that Jews from all over the world had gathered in Jerusalem to celebrate Pentecost. The Holy Spirit descended on the disciples, and they began to speak in other languages. The people gathered in the city, who were "from every nation under heaven," all heard the disciples speaking in their own native languages (Acts 2:1-11). Language was no longer a barrier to the people's ability to speak and hear about the mighty acts of God.

It's the reversal of Babel. The reconciling has begun.

We often recognize that the gospel is about restoring our unity with God. But what we don't often hear is that the gospel is also about restoring our unity with other human beings. But if that's true—if the gospel is about unity and solidarity among people—then the church ought to be a manifestation of that unity. So here's what this means for us: Our commitment to authentic Jesus-centered community is not optional, but it is absolutely foundational to our life with God and our witness to God's kingdom.

Of course, this is way easier said than done. Our culture worships at the altar of individualism. We are taught from an early age that it is all about "me"—my dreams, my goals, my ambitions, my rights, my wants, and my opinions. We really aren't given much of a chance to think any differently. It's one thing to value and celebrate people as individuals—there's nothing wrong with that. The problem comes when we worship the idea of the individual, when we elevate individuality so much that it becomes the beginning and end of one's identity. When we do that, we forget that our communities and relationships are indispensable parts of who we are.

Individualism naturally leads to isolation. Our mindset becomes: You have your life over there and I have my life over here, and as long as we respect each other's space everything will be just fine. The goal is to minimize our interaction with and dependence upon other people, or at least to control these things so that they happen on our terms. This shows up in so many ways. As an example, think about how we define convenience. Something is convenient if it allows us to avoid interacting with real human beings. We can go to the ATM and get money out of a machine, go through the self-checkout line at the grocery store, pay at the pump for gas, and then drive home without ever talking to another human being. And then we can go online and order a pizza—all in the name of convenience.

Think also about when we need help. For instance, we can imagine a couple who is having marital problems. *If* they seek out help, which is rare, typically they will go to a professional counselor who is outside of their common social circle so that they can keep things private. Don't get me wrong: I am a huge advocate for marital counseling and regularly urge couples to spend some time with professional counselors when it is needed. But very often there is a lack of transparency within a couple's circle of friends about the issues in their marriage. That lack of transparency can prevent the wisdom gained during the counseling sessions from sinking in and sticking around. A couple may experience some great breakthrough with their counselor, but what about when they go home? Who is going to walk with them from there to ensure that this new insight makes its way into their everyday life together? A community of friends can reinforce the counseling and support the couple as they work to strengthen their marriage. But very often, the individualistic ideal of privacy prevents the couple from receiving this valuable support.

The rampant individualism of our culture has crept its way into the church, and it has even deeply influenced how we understand salvation. One of my seminary professors gave a lecture on the role of community in the life of a follower of Jesus. He began the lecture by having the class discuss a quote first attributed to a third-century bishop named Saint Cyprian of Carthage: "Outside the church there is no salvation" (*Epistle LXXII, To Jubaianus, Concerning the Baptism of Heretics*). When the professor first put these words up on the projection screen, you could hear a collective gasp come from the people in the room. Everyone at my table immediately rejected this thought. As good western-minded Protestants, we were taught that salvation is by faith alone through grace alone, and all that was essential for salvation was that you accept Jesus into your heart. Apart from that you didn't need anything or anyone else in order to be saved. How could anyone say that the church is necessary for salvation?

The professor pointed out that how we respond to that quote has everything to do with what we believe about salvation. Often, we act as if salvation is just a one-time transaction between an individual and God so that he or she might receive forgiveness of sin and go to heaven. In that case, then no, the church isn't necessary for salvation.

But what if salvation is more than just forgiveness? What if salvation means a movement from forgiveness into wholeness? In that case, Cyprian is on to something with his words about the church. In 2 Corinthians 3:18, Paul speaks about this fuller aspect of salvation. He says that we are being transformed into the likeness of Christ, through the Spirit, "from one degree of glory to the next degree of glory." Salvation is nothing less than transformation, from glory into glory.

God wants to do more in our lives than just forgive us, as desperately as we need forgiveness and as good as it is to be assured of it. God also wants to make us whole—to bring us into the fullness of what it means to be a human being made in the image of God. The church is one of the primary ways in which God intends to do that. I like how Paul puts it in Ephesians Chapter 1. At the end of the chapter he says that the church "is the fullness of Christ, who fills everything in every way" (Ephesians 1:23).

Unfortunately, because of our individualistic bent and our tendency to isolate ourselves from one another, the communal aspects of our faith are treated as optional extracurricular activities. Maybe we will get around to them if we find the time, but we probably won't.

And we wonder why so *many* of us experience so *little* growth in our lives . . .

It's not that our faith isn't personal; it is deeply personal. The fullness of life in God begins with and is sustained by an intimate one-on-one connection with our Creator. But God's preferred way of working in us is through one another. Salvation is more than just forgiveness; it is also about transformation. In my experience, that sort of thing happens when people come together. Three Scripture passages will help us better understand how God works through us when we are together: 1 John 4:7-12; 3:16-18; and Hebrews 3:12-15.

God's Presence—1 John 4:7-12

Verse 12 is especially striking: "No one has ever seen God. If we love each other, God remains in us and his love is made perfect in us." That's one of those verses we ought to read slowly and then go back and read a few more times. We can't see God with our eyes nor can we reach out and touch God, but the author of First John tells us that when we come together and love one another, we experience the presence of God in a unique way.

The day after our honeymoon, my wife and I moved from South Carolina to Ohio in order to join the staff at a really great church where

I was to be one of the youth pastors. There we were, newlyweds, more than six hundred miles away from all of our friends and my wife's family. It wasn't an easy transition. There was, however, a family in Ohio that adopted us right from the start. They had several children involved in the church's ministry and they served as small group leaders, so we saw a lot of each other. They took us in as one of their own. They have one of those houses where the front door is never locked and people constantly come and go. There is always so much life and activity and noise in that house. It is a beautiful place.

One of my all time favorite memories was a July evening spent at this family's home. My wife's parents and my parents were all in town for a visit, and this church family had invited us all over for dinner. A bunch of high school students from the youth ministry had stopped over as well, and we were all sitting on blankets in the front yard telling stories and laughing until our throats were sore. I remember this one moment looking around and being taken aback at how beautiful it all was. God felt so close and everything just felt right—the way it should be.

We experience the presence of God most fully when we are together with our fellow believers, connected to one another and to Christ through love.

God's Provision—1 John 3:16-18

The author of First John isn't holding back with this one. One of the ways the love of God should manifest itself among followers of Jesus is in our willingness and commitment to provide for one another.

Several years ago, we were a part of a small group with some other couples. Not long after we had started meeting together, things got real. In a moment of vulnerability, one of the wives began to open up about some of the struggles they were experiencing. They had both just graduated from college, and she was struggling to find a job. At the same time, their student loan payments were starting to kick in, which was making it hard for them to get on their feet. To top it all off, the only car they owned had just broken down. As the wife was sharing this with us, you could tell the husband was surprised that she would lay all it all out there with a bunch of people they were just getting to know. We could all sense the overwhelming anxiety they felt, as well as and their uncertainty about what they should do next. The wife simply asked us to pray for them, which we did. But that wasn't all that the group did. The prayers moved some members of the group to action.

Over the next week, a member of the group took an extra car that they owned to an auto mechanic to make sure that everything was in working order. They put new tires on it and paid for the tags and registration. A few other people all pitched in and bought some gas cards. Then, anonymously, these group members gave it all to the couple. The husband shared with us afterwards that as much as he appreciated the car, more than anything the group's generosity was living proof that God hadn't forgotten about them.

That makes me wonder—who actually provided them with the car? Did God provide them with the car, or was it the group? If we take the words of First John seriously, the answer is simply, "yes." It's not an "either/or" kind of thing, but it is "both/and." God's faithfulness is often experienced through the faithfulness of God's people. Another aspect of our life with God that we experience more fully together is God's provision.

God's Work In Us—Hebrews 3:12-15

Well that seems a bit much don't you think? The author is telling us that somehow it is our responsibility to make sure that no one has an unbelieving heart, becomes hardened by sin's deceitfulness, or abandons our original convictions. How's that going for you?

The truth is, however, that we need one another to keep us on the right path. In that respect, it is up to my neighbor to help keep me from sin, and vice versa. One of my friends used to say that his mind was like a bad neighborhood; he didn't like going in there alone. God does his best work in us through the people we share our life with.

I remember watching a group of men support someone struggling with an addiction to an over-the-counter medication. It wasn't an actual narcotic, so it was easy for him to rationalize it and write it off. The thing that bothered him, though, was that he was hiding it from his wife. Something felt wrong about that. So he shared this with the group in order to get some wisdom from them about what he should do. They helped him to see that what he was feeling was conviction from the Holy Spirit; he needed to respond to it. Yes, there were more dangerous substances to which he could be addicted, but its like the author of Hebrews says: "If you hear his voice, don't have stubborn hearts" (3:15). Continuing to rationalize his addiction could cause him to become deaf to God's voice. At the same time, he was purposefully keeping something from his wife, planting a seed of mistrust that could grow into something much more destructive. Because of the group's support he eventually told his wife and gave up the addiction. It wasn't easy, but he is a better man and his marriage is stronger because of that group's commitment to encourage him in staying true to the Spirit's conviction.

G. K. Chesterton said it like this: "Thinking in isolation and with pride ends in being an idiot (*Orthodoxy*, Barnes and Noble, 2007 [original 1908]; page 34)." Isn't that the truth? God often works in us through other people, using the community to help us identify and commit to doing the next right thing.

There is a depth to our life with God that we can only experience when we come together, when we are one. Sometimes we find ourselves asking, "Where is God?" Perhaps a better question for us to ask is "Where are we?" Where are we in regards to our commitment to one another? When we cut ourselves off from community, we simultaneously separate ourselves from some of the primary ways in which God works in our lives. The most important thing for us to know right now, as we journey toward a shared life, is that our involvement with Christ-centered community is not optional; it is absolutely foundational.

I say all of this because there will be moments when you will want to quit. Don't. There will be times when you will wonder if it is worth it. It is. The kind of intimacy we long for with one another doesn't happen overnight. Often our commitment to work through the discomfort and frustration of truly loving one another is the very thing that God will use to bring us closer.

You are also going to have moments when you experience the living God together. You will have moments when heaven and earth will seem to meet in your very midst, and you will be keenly aware that the space you share together is holy ground. Recognize and name those moments, call them out, and remember them. They will serve as the proof you need to know that life is so much better when we live it together as one.

IN YOUR GROUP

Starting Out

Central to this study is the belief that God has created humans to exist in relationship with one another. Each participant in your group comes from a different background and has a different story. These unique qualities have shaped each of you over time. In order to begin to build a strong relational connection among yourselves, take time to ask one another the questions listed below. While one person from the group is answering, challenge yourself to be an active listener and engage with their responses. It's important to take a few minutes to get to know one another from the very beginning.

1. What is your name? Where are you from? What would you like to share about your family or home life?

2. What do you hope to accomplish by being a part of this ONE study?

The Three Questions

There are three questions with which you will become very familiar during your time in this study. At the beginning of each week's meeting, you'll answer one or more of these questions. You'll also spend some time reflecting on them individually throughout the week. These questions are meant to give everyone in the group common language to be able to share where they are in their spiritual journey and what God is doing in their lives. We will spend some time talking about the role these questions can play in the life of your group, but first let's familiarize ourselves with them.

The Three Questions are:

1. What are you grateful for?

2. What are you anxious about?

3. What are you learning?

Everyone in the group should answer whichever question is easiest for you to answer right now. The more familiar you get with asking them of yourselves and sharing them with one another, the easier this will be.

Study the Scriptures

Read Acts 2:42-47 and 4:32-37 on the next two pages. Make notes on the following questions in the space provided there.

1. What parts of the community described in these verses do you find attractive? Why?

2. What characteristics of these early believers do you find in both passages?

3. What does it mean to live in community with "one heart and mind"?

4. What makes this type of community so elusive in our culture today?

Acts 2:42-47

[42]The believers devoted themselves to the apostles' teaching, to the community, to their shared meals, and to their prayers. [43]A sense of awe came over everyone. God performed many wonders and signs through the apostles. [44]All the believers were united and shared everything. [45]They would sell pieces of property and possessions and distribute the proceeds to everyone who needed them. [46]Every day, they met together in the temple and ate in their homes. They shared food with gladness and simplicity. [47]They praised God and demonstrated God's goodness to everyone. The Lord added daily to the community those who were being saved.

Acts 4:32-37

[32]The community of believers was one in heart and mind. None of them would say, "This is mine!" about any of their possessions, but held everything in common. [33]The apostles continued to bear powerful witness to the resurrection of the Lord Jesus, and an abundance of grace was at work among them all. [34]There were no needy persons among them. Those who owned properties or houses would sell them, bring the proceeds from the sales, [35]and place them in the care and under the authority of the apostles. Then it was distributed to anyone who was in need.

[36]Joseph, whom the apostles nicknamed Barnabas (that is, "one who encourages"), was a Levite from Cyprus. [37] He owned a field, sold it, brought the money, and placed it in the care and under the authority of the apostles.

The Allure of Individualism

The allure of individualism seems to affect every part of our lives. On the next four pages, write or draw the ways it is evident in each of the following areas. What contributes to and perpetuates the problem? Then plan to discuss with the group as a whole.

FAMILY

FRIENDSHIP

WORKPLACE

FAITH COMMUNITY

Experiencing God Together

Read 1 John 4:7-12; 1 John 3:16-18; and Hebrews 3:12-15. In each of these passages, what are some aspects of our life with God that we experience more fully together as opposed to on our own? Write or draw your responses in the space provided.

1 John 4:7-12

[7]Dear friends, let's love each other, because love is from God, and everyone who loves is born from God and knows God. [8]The person who doesn't love does not know God, because God is love. [9]This is how the love of God is revealed to us: God has sent his only Son into the world so that we can live through him. [10]This is love: it is not that we loved God but that he loved us and sent his Son as the sacrifice that deals with our sins.

[11]Dear friends, if God loved us this way, we also ought to love each other. [12]No one has ever seen God. If we love each other, God remains in us and his love is made perfect in us.

1 John 3:16-18

[16]This is how we know love: Jesus laid down his life for us, and we ought to lay down our lives for our brothers and sisters. [17]But if a person has material possessions and sees a brother or sister in need and that person doesn't care—how can the love of God remain in him?

[18]Little children, let's not love with words or speech but with action and truth.

Hebrews 3:12-15

[12]Watch out, brothers and sisters, so that none of you have an evil, unfaithful heart that abandons the living God. [13]Instead, encourage each other every day, as long as it's called "today," so that none of you become insensitive to God because of sin's deception. [14]We are partners with Christ, but only if we hold on to the confidence we had in the beginning until the end.

[15]When it says,

Today, if you hear his voice, don't have stubborn hearts
  as they did in the rebellion.

ONE CHALLENGE

Relationships are organic, and therefore they must be birthed and sustained with intention. This week's challenge is for you to spend some one-on-one time together with one other person in your group. Set this meeting in your calendars, and choose a good location for conversation, such as a coffee shop, a restaurant, or a park. During your time together, focus on getting to know each other's history. What is the other person's family like? What are her hobbies? Where did he grow up? Where has she traveled? Start with generalities and let the conversation grow deeper as it continues. Make special note of the way you see God involved in your interaction. Commit to praying for the other person throughout this week.

I'm meeting with:_____

DEVOTIONAL

A Word About Those Three Questions . . .

Jesus' prayer in John 17 wasn't that his followers would spend an hour and some change sitting shoulder to shoulder with a bunch of strangers, but that we would be brought to complete unity. What Jesus had in mind wasn't some distanced association based on proximity, but a oneness that is the result of sharing our lives with one another.

I have to wonder: How prepared are you to do that? I don't mean your willingness (we will get to that later), but more so in your awareness. You can't share what you don't know. How aware are you of your life—namely where God is and what God is up to in you, around you, and through you?

That's what these questions are here for. Asking them of yourself on a regular basis is one way in which you can grow in your awareness of the work God is doing and the work God still needs to do in you.

I want to encourage you not just to wrestle with them once a week when you are asked to answer them, but to ruminate on them daily. This isn't about answering a question correctly on a pop quiz. It is about developing a practice of awareness, growing in intimacy with God, and opening ourselves up to one another.

I also want to challenge you to move past vague generalities. If you are grateful for your job, be more specific. What is it about your job you are grateful for? Dig a little deeper. The goal is to open our eyes to the presence of a very real God and to become more and more aware of the life that we are living. One of the ways this happens is by doing the hard work of looking for the answers to these questions in the details of our everyday lives.

Following the next three sessions, there will be a weeklong devotional that will focus on each of the three questions and explore the role it plays in our life with God. I can imagine that some of us struggle with a regular practice of reading and reflecting on the Scriptures and have been meaning to start such a practice. Now is as good a time as any. The Bible can be a confusing book and often leaves us with more questions than answers. The good news is you will have a group of people to share those questions with.

These devotionals are designed to help you ask these questions of yourself and better prepare you to share with your group. So what do you say we get started with that first question: "What are you grateful for?"

What are you grateful for?

At the heart of our faith is this thing called grace. Grace is a gift— undeserved, unmerited, unending gift. Everything God has done and continues to do for us in Jesus is one giant on-going gift that we cannot earn or achieve. We can only accept and receive. There is only one proper way to respond to grace, and that is to be grateful. Gratitude is the posture of someone who has truly embraced the grace and goodness of God.

It's one thing to say God is good. Its quite another to actually believe it. Identifying the gifts in our lives is what leads us into joy, an unwavering awareness and trust in God's presence and goodness.

Joy transcends our circumstances, and it does not come and go. It is the result of an on-going practice of gratitude. It comes when we abide in the wonderful truth of the gospel and see, name, and respond to the gifts of God we are surrounded by all of the time.

This week's devotional will lead us to what the Scriptures have to say about the relationship between gratitude and joy. It will help make us more ready to answer the question, "What are you grateful for?"

Day 1

Read Psalm 28

What does this psalm have to say about joy? Where does joy come from? What does it mean that the psalmist's heart rejoiced? Have you ever had an experience like that? What was it like?

Day 2

Read Psalm 30

What does this psalm teach us about joy? What does it mean to be clothed with joy? What is the relationship between joy and repentance?

Day 3

Read Psalm 51

In this psalm, the author actually asks for joy. What does that say about the nature of joy?

Is there some sort of despair that you are dealing with that is stealing your joy? Name it, and then make this psalm your prayer today.

Day 4

Read Psalm 65

According to this psalm, where is joy? What does this teach us about the nature of joy? What role do we play in experiencing joy? Make a list of the various people in your life for whom you are grateful.

Day 5

Read Philippians 4:4-9

Read through these verses carefully. What is the relationship between joy, thanksgiving, anxiety, and peace? What are some of your own personal anxieties? How does running them through the flow of thought offered in this passage bring you peace?

Day 6

Read 1 Thessalonians 1:1-10; Philippians 4:4-9

How can joy exist alongside suffering? When have you experienced joy in the midst of trial? What did you learn? How did you grow? How has that experience shaped the way you view difficulties now?

Day 7

Read 1 Peter 1:1-25

According to verses 8-9, what is the ultimate reason for our joy? How aware are you of your soul's need for salvation? How does grounding yourself in the truth of this Scripture affect your joy?

Session 2:

ONE MIND

I am from Indianapolis, and as a result, I am huge Indianapolis Colts fan. Naturally, that means I cannot stand the New England Patriots. If you know anything about the NFL, then you are somewhat aware of this rivalry. Well, several years ago my wife and I were given tickets to the annual Colts/Patriots game in Indianapolis. The seats were amazing, and the game was even better.

The Colts were getting hammered in the first half—I'm pretty sure they were down by like twenty-one points. But in the second half they started to come back, and eventually, they won the game on a last-second pass that Reggie Wayne caught right in front of us.

When he caught that pass, the crowd went absolutely crazy. There were nearly sixty-five thousand people there, and they were all cheering with happiness. I remember this little old lady—who had been sitting right next to me the entire game and barely said a word—grabbing my shoulders and screaming in my face. There was even this guy sitting one section over from us who was on his knees weeping. He wasn't just shedding a few tears, but literally sobbing.

There is this sort of energy we experience when we are in the midst of a group of people who are all gathered around the same passion or who are pursuing the same purpose. The same thing happens at a concert. You've probably been there before, in the midst of a huge crowd of people all singing their favorite songs together. Just thinking about it makes the hairs on my neck stand up.

It happens after a tragedy as well. I remember after 9/11 seeing all of these unbelievable expressions of solidarity, and for a brief period of time, the entire nation came together in a really beautiful way.

Here is when we begin to see what separates a crowd from a community. A crowd is a group of people who have all gathered in the same place at the same time, but a community is a bit different. A community is a group of people who have gathered not just in the same place, but around the same purpose. At that Colts game, I got a glimpse of what happens when a crowd briefly transforms into a community.

The church isn't to be just any sort of community—it is to be the truest sense of community. All other forms of community tap into our fundamental and innate desires for connection and camaraderie, but it's like Paul says in the Letter to the Colossians—they are all just shadows, but the reality is found in Christ (Colossians 2:17).

We have been looking to the early church as our example as we pursue a shared life together. The Book of Acts tells us that this community of Jesus' followers was of one heart and one mind. These people were from all over the world; they all had different ways of doing things, a variety of customs and backgrounds. I think it's safe to assume that they didn't see eye to eye on everything, but they all had this life-changing experience, and through the power of the Holy Spirit they became one.

In this session, we will explore what it means to be of one mind, to move past just being a crowd and into a community: a group of people gathered around not just any purpose, but the greatest purpose—the good news of Jesus Christ and the kingdom of God.

When I say that the early church had "one mind," what I mean is that they were united around the same purpose. It's important that we recognize clearly what common purpose held the early church together. The passage in Acts Chapter 4 tells us that purpose: "The apostles continued to bear powerful witness to the resurrection of the Lord Jesus" (Acts 4:33). Now the resurrection wasn't just Jesus' last and greatest miracle; it was also an act of vindication. It was proof that God had lifted Jesus up and established him as the true Lord of the world. When the Holy Spirit descends on the apostles, Peter tells the crowd of onlookers that Jesus was raised from the dead (Acts 2:22-36). Peter concludes with the following words about the meaning of the Resurrection: "Therefore, let all Israel know beyond question that God has made this Jesus, whom you crucified, both Lord and Christ" (Acts 2:36).

The Christ, or Messiah, was the one whom the prophets foretold would usher in the kingdom of God. At this time in history, the people of Israel were used to being kicked around and oppressed. For most of the previous six centuries, each of the world's great empires had ruled over them one after another. But the prophets said that it wouldn't always be like this. One day, the Messiah would come and would set things right, not just for Israel but for all people, because this Messiah would establish the reign of God over the whole world. The prophet Isaiah describes it like this:

> But here is my servant, the one I uphold;
>   my chosen, who brings me delight.
> I've put my spirit upon him;
>   he will bring justice to the nations.
> He won't cry out or shout aloud
>   or make his voice heard in public.
> He won't break a bruised reed;
>   he won't extinguish a faint wick,
>   but he will surely bring justice.
> He won't be extinguished or broken
>   until he has established justice in the land.
> The coastlands await his teaching. (Isaiah 42:1-4)

The proclamation of God's kingdom was the central theme of all of Jesus' teachings. In fact, the phrase "kingdom of God" or "kingdom of heaven" shows up more than eighty times in the Gospels. That's a whole lot of kingdom talk. But Jesus' meaning was different than what we might think. Our English word *kingdom* tends to make us think of a geographical place, such as the United Kingdom or the Magic Kingdom. The Greek word that occurs in the Gospels, *basileia*, can mean a geographical territory. But more often it means rule or reign. It usually refers to royal power or the act of ruling, which means it's more about authority than locality. So when Jesus says "kingdom of God" or "kingdom of heaven," he doesn't mean a specific place. He means the rule or the reign of God.

According to Peter's proclamation in Acts 2, the Resurrection is what definitively proved that Jesus was in fact both Lord and Messiah. This means the Resurrection wasn't just some sort of attention-grabbing magic trick in order to get the people's attention. It was the decisive victory in an invasion. The kingdom of God was breaking into the world.

In Acts 4, Luke tells us that the apostles continued to testify to the Resurrection not just with words, but with great power. They didn't just tell people about what they had experienced. Their lives, both individually and communally, bore "powerful witness" to Jesus' resurrection (verse 33). The community of believers was the very place where the kingdom of God was advancing, where heaven was crashing to earth. Tell me, who doesn't want in on that? The common purpose that held the early church together was bearing witness to the Resurrection, demonstrating the kingdom of God in their very midst. Insofar as they shared this purpose, they were of one mind.

Let me pause here and say a quick word on what being of one mind *doesn't* mean. It most certainly doesn't mean that everyone has to think the same or agree on everything. Christ-centered community is about unity, not uniformity. Paul tells us that the church is a body made up of different parts, but all coming together to act as one (1 Corinthians 12:12-26).

One of the most beautiful things about the church is that we all come from different places, each with our own perspective on things and our own experiences. And that's OK. Much of the New Testament consists of letters written to actual churches, made up of real people, who dealt with controversies and disagreements in their communities. How shocking! In Romans 14, Paul counseled the Roman church about some of the disagreements they were having, which involved certain foods, special days, and people's specific beliefs and convictions. What is interesting is that Paul doesn't spend any time discussing which side is right and which side is wrong. Instead he tells them to make every effort to live in peace, not to pass judgment on one another, and to keep their personal convictions between themselves and God. Paul expected that the community could maintain disagreement about food and drink, because "God's kingdom isn't about eating food and drinking but about righteousness, peace, and joy in the Holy Spirit" (Romans 14:17).

Being of one mind doesn't mean that we all have to agree. In fact, our commitment to a greater purpose—the ultimate purpose, Christ—is what frees us up to be able to disagree about lesser things and still remain one.

To take it a step further, more often than not the difficultly of being in community with those who are "different" is that we simply don't like it. We don't like being challenged by those who have a different view from us, and frustration often arises when we truly try to love them. But in truth, this frustration and commitment to *love* those whom we don't always *like* is the very thing that God uses to shape us into the likeness of Jesus.

For the early church, their purpose was clear. Everyone knew why they were all there and what they were about. They existed to bear witness to the Resurrection and the reign of God in the world. This is where their life as individuals was found and what their shared life together was about.

Now, let's talk about us, the church today. Here is where we begin to address one of the biggest reasons why so many small-group communities struggle to get off the ground: No one really knows why they are there or what the group is about.

Sure, most groups begin with everyone feeling compelled to be in a small group. Maybe the pastor or other leadership of the church convinces them that it's important, or perhaps friends invite them or even drag them there, or they respond to their own innate sense that it's something they need. Once everyone shows up, however, there is no conversation about the greater question: "Why?" As a result, many groups never moved out of what I like to call "the awkward first-date stage." Typically, the group will limp along for a few weeks until everyone decides that it's just not that important or that it isn't working and they quit.

Or something else can happen. The group won't fizzle out, but the members will end up committing themselves to a lesser purpose than Jesus Christ. In that case it's really easy for the group to become just another get-together.

If you are anything like me, that's not what I need. In fact, I don't have time for just another get-together. I need to connect with a group of people who are going to challenge me to be more and do more than I thought was possible, people with whom I can celebrate the beauty of life, who will be there for me when it all falls apart, and who can partner with me to influence the world around us. I believe that is what Jesus wants and expects of us as well. Only when we have a common commitment to our purpose—bearing witness to the resurrection of Jesus—can we truly be of one mind.

So how do we do our part in order for us to be of one mind? We can go back to Acts and see what we can learn from the people who did it first.

In Acts, Luke gives us a pretty in-depth look at how the community lived together, along with the various disciplines and activities they were committed to. When we consider these disciplines and activities as a whole, we can group them into three large, core practices that are absolutely essential for Christ-centered community. These core practices are: pushing one another forward; lifting one another up; and sending one another out.

Pushing One Another Forward

In Acts Chapter 2, we are told that the believers were devoted to the apostles' teaching (Acts 2:42). The community wasn't only concerned with sharing the gospel with others; they were also committed to reflecting on and responding to the further implications the gospel made on their lives. They were open to instruction and growth, allowing the grace of God to penetrate further and further into their lives. One of the core practices that characterized the early church was pushing one another forward in this way.

We see this core practice even in the Gospels when Jesus is still with the disciples. In Matthew 18, Jesus says to his followers: "If your brother or sister sins against you, go and correct them when you are alone together. If they listen to you, then you've won over your brother or sister" (Matthew 18:15). When we read this teaching, our tendency is to get caught up in the specifics and jump right to how to apply it in the church. When we do this, however, we miss a huge assumption that Jesus is making concerning our relationships. In this statement, Jesus assumes that his followers have relationships with one another that allow them to do this sort of thing. Jesus takes it for granted that his followers can point out one another's sins and nobody is going to freak out. Nobody will become defensive or write each other off as being judgmental.

Let me ask you, do you have that? Because I have found that it is actually quite rare, and it is one of the biggest reasons why so many of us experience so little growth in our lives.

I once led a small group with some guys that I worked out with at a gym in my area. We had been working out together for a while and seemed to get along, so I pitched them the idea of carving out some time for us to talk about the things that matter most to us. They all liked the sound of that, and a small group was formed. I will never forget our first morning together. In a moment of transparency, one of the guys I had known for a while said, "I have been going to church for such a long time, but if I'm honest I don't feel like anything has really changed in my life." Here I was thinking we would just ease into things! In response to his statement, several of the other guys admitted the same thing. I asked them if they had ever been committed to something like what we were doing that morning: a group of guys they could be honest with and open up to. They all said no. After a few weeks together, we all began to experience growth in our lives as we challenged and encouraged one another to pursue more in our life with God. One of them men even began to work toward reconnecting with his brother whom he had not spoken to for a couple of years.

It's very easy for us to become stagnant in our spiritual lives when we try to grow alone. But when we push one another forward, we all grow toward God together. This is what Jesus had in mind when he taught his followers to correct one another, and it's what the early church did when they devoted themselves to the apostles' teachings. It requires a lot of hard work, commitment, and trust for us to establish relationships in which we can do this. But this is how we grow as disciples of Jesus.

Lifting One Another Up

The community of Jesus followers in Acts was not only dedicated to pushing one another forward, they were also diligent in lifting one another up.

This early church in Jerusalem was made up of people who had come into the city from all over the world in order to celebrate Pentecost. While they were in Jerusalem, they had a life-altering encounter with the Spirit of Christ (Acts 2:1-41). There was no way they could just go back home right away as if nothing extraordinary had happened. They needed some time to sort all this out and to understand the implications of what had happened. But where were they going to stay? How were they going to eat? Nearly everything they owned was hundreds of miles away. In Chapter 2, we read about the church's response to this situation: The believers would actually sell their possessions in order to "distribute the proceeds to everyone who needed them" (Acts 2:45). It seems that the believers who were from the area gave what they had in order to make sure their brothers and sisters were taken care of. The description in Chapter 4 goes on to say that there were no needy persons among them (Acts 4:34), and as we saw last session, that's a sign of God's power at work among them. This was a group of people who quite simply took care of one another—who lifted one another up by meeting one another's needs.

A couple of years ago some dear friends of mine experienced a horrific tragedy in their family. Their twenty-year-old son was hit by a speeding SUV while crossing the street. A small group of us spent that entire night with the family in the hospital waiting room, praying with the family and jumping out of our seats every time someone came through the double doors. We weren't sure if he was going to make it. Miraculously, he did make it; but as a result of the accident, he is now paralyzed from the waist down. This hasn't stopped him from living his life. This young man will forever be one of my greatest heroes. He is one of the clearest pictures I have of courage and resilience, and I am a better person for knowing him.

It was so inspiring to watch the way the community around this family responded to what had happened. Their needs were met in just about every way imaginable. People from the community brought them meals. Some of them watched the younger children so the parents could stay in the hospital with their injured son. Others cleaned the house and kept up with the yard work during this time. Someone from the community organized a renovation project to make the house wheelchair accessible. They even transformed the family's garage into a new apartment for the young man to live in when he came home.

Tell me, how well do you think this family would have fared if they had had to go through this tragedy and major life transition on their own? Thankfully, they will never have to answer that question, because the whole community gathered around them to lift them up during their time of need.

A core practice of Christ-centered community is the practice of lifting one another up. When we provide for one another in our times and places of need, it helps us remain of one mind and purpose.

Sending One Another Out

Luke tells us in Acts Chapter 2 that this group of Jesus followers "demonstrated God's goodness to everyone" (Acts 2:47). While the CEB uses this wording, the NRSV more accurately captures the meaning of the Greek by saying the Christians enjoyed "the goodwill of all the people" (Acts 2:47 NRSV). That word *goodwill* means that the people were favorably disposed towards the early Christians, showing them respect and recognizing something good within them. In other words, something about these Jesus followers was attractive, winning over the people around them. And of course, "all the people" literally means "all the people." The whole city of Jerusalem responded well to the community of believers.

Think about that for a moment. The entire city respected and admired these Christians. Tell me, who are the people you respect and admire? The ones who stay as far away from you as possible, who try to avoid you like you have a disease, or who look down on you? No.

The people whom we respect and admire are those who have in some way made a positive impact on our lives or our communities. They are the people who serve, who contribute, who make their communities and others' lives better. When Luke says that Jesus' followers had the goodwill of all the people, he means that these people made the city a better place. Even those who were not a part of the Christian movement were glad those followers of Jesus were there in their midst.

The third core practice of Christ-centered community is sending one another out. When we are of one mind, united around Resurrection and the good news of the kingdom of God, then whatever happens inside the group ought to make an impact on the world outside of the group. The group ensures that this happens by sending each other out, seeing and responding to the needs of others together.

I know of a couple that felt called by God to open up their home and become foster parents. Over the past several years, they have had numerous children come into their home, some for long stays and others for shorter periods of time. Almost all of those children came out of terrible living situations and lacked any sort of positive picture of a loving family. The couple has three biological children of their own, which makes the situations even more complicated.

Some of the foster children have pushed this family to the edge and made them question God's calling on their life. From kids trying to run away to profanity-saturated tirades, this family constantly wrestles with a feeling of tension between protecting their biological children and loving and serving their foster children.

Thankfully, this family is surrounded by a community that is devoted to the practice of sending one another out. The members of their small group constantly remind them of God's call on their life. When they are wondering if they are getting anywhere, they remind them of the breakthroughs and the life-altering experiences some of the children have had in their home. When they grow weary of the sacrifice it requires of them and their family, the group reminds them of all the ways in which they have changed for the better. The group doesn't only encourage the couple to continue loving their foster children even when things are hard. The group loves the foster children too, welcoming them into their own lives and contributing to the couple's calling.

They could be just another middle-class family holed up inside their three-bedroom house, preoccupied with trying to keep their own kids safe. But the group sends them out. Because of the people they share life with, these people are miracle workers, influencing the life trajectory of the kids most of the world forgets about. Their home itself is sent out into the world, because its doors are open. It is a home in every sense of the word. Because the group sends them out, this family is caught up not just in any purpose, but in the greatest purpose: the good news of Jesus Christ and the kingdom of God.

The Covenant Statement

These are the three core practices of Christ-centered communities: pushing one another forward, lifting one another up, and sending one another out. These core practices help ensure that we stay of one mind, gathered around the right purpose, and bear a common witness to the Resurrection.

It is absolutely essential for you to discuss what shape these core practices will take in your small-group community. During the next several weeks, you will be led through various exercises that will help you develop a covenant statement concerning these three core practices. Your covenant statement will express your particular group's commitment to the three core practices, establishing exactly how you will push one another forward, lift one another up, and send one another out.

I've had the opportunity to officiate a couple of wedding vow renewal ceremonies. In these moments, I could clearly see the power these vows have on reminding us what a marriage commitment truly is. When we first get married, it is easy for the wedding vows to blend into the background amid the hoopla of the celebration. But the vows take center stage when a couple comes together to recommit themselves to one another, especially after thirty years and half a lifetime of ups and downs, joys and struggles. On days like that the vows reveal what it is required of both parties in order to be true to their covenant relationship and experience a beautiful marriage together. The truth is, those vows could stand to be repeated and renewed on a daily basis.

In a way, that is the role this covenant statement will play in the life of your small group. It will act as your rallying point, the place you come back to when it seems like the group is spinning its wheels or has lost its way. I strongly encourage you to set some time aside once or twice a year to discuss how well the group is being true to the covenant statement and to recommit yourselves to the three core practices.

It is also vitally important for these covenant statements to be specific to each group. These three core practices will flesh themselves out uniquely in our various contexts. Pushing one another forward, lifting one another up, and sending one another out may look a bit different in a group made up of young families as opposed to a group that consists of empty nesters.

At the same time, having some skin in the game helps to create a sense of ownership. The energy spent discussing and wrestling with how these practices will actually manifest themselves in the community will only help to clarify what the group is about and how the group will function.

You know, as incredible as my experience was at that Colts game, it was also a sobering reality check. Yes, we were sixty-five thousand people all united around the same purpose. But that purpose was a game. I couldn't help but wonder, "What if we were this passionate about something that actually mattered?" What if we were that devoted to spurring one another on to being the kind of people God intends us to be? What if we were that committed to meeting one another's needs? What if we were that concerned with seeing the world changed? What would that be like? I love sports, especially football, but in the end it is just a game. The reality is that some of the things we are most passionate about and the most devoted to really aren't all that important. As the church, we have been called to center our lives around the greatest passion and purpose the world has ever known: the Kingdom of God, God's perfect reign here on earth, the renewal and healing of all things. If we are going to come together, lets make sure it's around nothing less than that.

IN YOUR GROUP

The Three Questions

Relationships can form and grow deeper only when we invest time and energy in them. During the second week of your ONE experience, it is important that you work to continue developing close, personal relationships with those in your group. Before you dive into this week's study, take time as a group to answer the first of the three questions:

1. What are you grateful for?

2. What are you anxious about?

3. What are you learning?

Study the Scriptures

Read Acts 2:42-47 and Acts 4:32-37 on the following pages. Make notes on your responses to the questions below in the space provided there.

1. How would you describe the kind of connection among the believers that we see in these two passages?

2. Share a time when you have experienced this kind of connection with other people.

3. What words, phrases, or verses do you think best summarize the purpose around which the early church was gathered?

Acts 2:42-47

[42]The believers devoted themselves to the apostles' teaching, to the community, to their shared meals, and to their prayers. [43]A sense of awe came over everyone. God performed many wonders and signs through the apostles. [44]All the believers were united and shared everything. [45]They would sell pieces of property and possessions and distribute the proceeds to everyone who needed them. [46]Every day, they met together in the temple and ate in their homes. They shared food with gladness and simplicity. [47]They praised God and demonstrated God's goodness to everyone. The Lord added daily to the community those who were being saved.

Acts 4:32-37

[32]The community of believers was one in heart and mind. None of them would say, "This is mine!" about any of their possessions, but held everything in common. [33]The apostles continued to bear powerful witness to the resurrection of the Lord Jesus, and an abundance of grace was at work among them all. [34]There were no needy persons among them. Those who owned properties or houses would sell them, bring the proceeds from the sales, [35]and place them in the care and under the authority of the apostles. Then it was distributed to anyone who was in need.

[36]Joseph, whom the apostles nicknamed Barnabas (that is, "one who encourages"), was a Levite from Cyprus. [37]He owned a field, sold it, brought the money, and placed it in the care and under the authority of the apostles.

Pushing One Another Forward

Draw or write your responses to the questions below.

1. What comes to your mind when you think of pushing one another forward?

2. Name a time when someone pushed you forward or when, looking back now, you wish they had?

3. What was your relationship with this person? What made you receptive to their efforts to help you grow? What enabled them to step up to push you forward?

4. Be honest about your spiritual growth lately. How is your life changing as a result of following Jesus?

5. How do you need others in this group to help push you forward in your relationship with God?

6. How can you push someone else forward?

Lifting One Another Up

Draw or write your responses to the questions below.

1. What stories or situations come to mind when you think of lifting one another up?

2. Name some situations that might require the group to lift someone up.

3. Name a time when you wish someone had lifted you up.

4. Name a time when someone did lift you up.

5. How do you need to be lifted up right now?

Sending One Another Out

Draw or write your responses to the questions below.

  1. What comes to mind when you think of sending one another out?

  2. Why is sending one another out such an important practice for groups to exercise?

3. Name a time when you wish someone had sent you out.

4. Name a time when someone did send you out.

ONE CHALLENGE

This week, prayerfully put one of these new practices into action. Seek God's guidance in discerning who in your group needs to be pushed forward, lifted up, or sent out. Choose an appropriate way to accomplish your practice of choice. Consider texting someone, writing a card, meeting face-to-face, or purchasing a gift.

DEVOTIONAL

What are you anxious about?

Anxious. Chances are that when you hear that word, various things come to mind. It may be personal fears and insecurities, or some sort of need you have, or a situation that feels, for whatever reason, out of your control. Being anxious is about feeling pulled apart, scattered, or fragmented.

You know this. It's when someone is talking to you and you are there physically, but your mind is somewhere else. Or it's when you're laying in bed at night but you're not asleep because your mind won't quiet down.

More often than not our anxieties reveal one of two things. Either we are placing our trust in something apart from God—so other people's opinions, a fear of failing, or some sense of inadequacy is getting the best of us—or we have a very real need that requires some serious and practical attention. What we have to understand is that we receive both freedom and comfort when we share these things with other people.

In one sense, when we share our anxieties we are practicing the discipline of confession; we are acknowledging that something is off, that something isn't right. Sharing this and getting it out in the open is the first step to seeing our anxiety resolved. At the same time, the group may often be the vessel through which God wants to meet our need.

Day 1

Read 2 Corinthians 1:1-11

How does this passage speak to our willingness to share our anxieties with one another? What role does the community play in seeing them resolved? How does this passage encourage you? How does it challenge you?

Day 2

Read Psalm 32

How can keeping silent about sin make it feel like your bones are wasting away? How do you relate to that? What does this psalm say about the power of confession?

Day 3

Read James 5:13-20

Why is it important to confess our sins to one another? What does this accomplish in addition to our confessions to God? What does this passage have to say about the gift we are to one another?

Day 4

Read John 8:1-11

How do you think the woman in this passage was feeling about herself before Jesus intervened? How do you think she felt about herself walking away from Jesus? How does this passage empower us to own our failures?

Day 5

Read Psalm 51

What does this psalm have to teach us about the practice and power of confession? How does it challenge you personally? How does it encourage you?

Day 6

Read Luke 15:1-32

Quite often we allow guilt and condemnation to drive us away from God. What does the story of the Prodigal Son have to say about that? How would seeing God as a loving Father empower us to deal with our dysfunction?

Day 7

Read 1 John 3:11-24

What does this passage have to say about the role the community plays in dealing with our anxieties? Are there any practical needs you have that the group can meet? Is there a practical need you are aware of that you have the means to meet?

Session 3:

ONE HEART

I n Acts Chapter 4, we read that this early group of Jesus followers was not only of one mind, but they were also of one heart. The word *heart* isn't talking about the organ in our chest that pumps blood. It refers to that innermost part of who we are, or what some scholars refer to as the center of our being.

For the early church, this sacred part of their lives wasn't something that was off limits from one another, but it was involved and incorporated in their shared life together. Not only was there a singleness of mind, but there was a depth of heart as well.

In this session, we will explore what it means to be of one heart—to move past surface level relationships and into chest-deep, authentic community.

Again, our scriptural starting point will be Acts Chapters 2 and 4. Toward the end of Luke's description in Acts Chapter 2, he sneaks in a comment that is easy to miss, but it captures the essence of what it means to be of one heart. In verse 46, he tells us that, "Every day they met together in the temple and ate in their homes. They shared food with gladness and simplicity."

Just like today, but to a much greater degree in the ancient world, sharing a meal in someone's home was an expression of community. Food was a precious resource. In our day and age, and in our part of the world, we tend to take having enough food to eat for granted. We have more than enough food, but we are not better off for it. A fact sheet by the United Nations Environment Programme includes the troubling statistic that in the United States, roughly 30-40 percent of our food supply is wasted—it is simply discarded (from "Food Waste: The Facts," *www.worldfooddayusa.org/food_waste_the_facts*). At the same time, a researcher at the National Institute of Health estimates that just a quarter of that wasted food would be enough to provide three meals a day for around 43 million people (From *American Wasteland: How America Throws Away Nearly Half of Its Food* [*And What We Can Do About It*], by Jonathan Bloom; Da Capo, 2010; pages 46-47).

It may be hard for us to truly appreciate the food in our refrigerators and pantries, but in reality it is an incredible blessing to have food on our tables. Food isn't something to be discarded; it must be cherished because it was a gift given by the Creator God in order to sustain life.

I believe the ancient Jews, and the Christians who grew out of that culture, understood the importance of food to a greater extent than we do today. To share something so valuable with others wasn't a casual thing for them; it was in fact an act of solidarity. That's why covenants or treaties—binding relationships of mutual obligation—were often ratified with a meal or feast (see Genesis 26:26-31; 31:43-55; Exodus 24:9-11). To eat a meal with someone was to identify with them—to allow them into your inner circle and make them a part of your tribe. That's also why there is so much fuss in the Gospels from the religious folks over whom Jesus eats with (Matthew 9:10-11; Mark 2:15-16; Luke 5:30). The religious leaders were bothered when Jesus ate with sinners and tax collectors, because by doing so Jesus, this man of God, was identifying with them.

For the earliest Christians, eating together daily wasn't about simply sharing food; it was a sharing of life. You see, being of one heart is a matter of allowing others to have a seat at your "table." It's about letting them into the inner most parts of who you are.

Notice what it says about the manner of their eating. Not only did they share a meal together, they ate "with gladness and simplicity." That word *simplicity* can also be understood as sincerity, meaning without pretense. In other words, there was no performance, no games in their daily meals. The believers were real with one another.

Are you feeling a bit uncomfortable with all of this? It doesn't exactly come easy for us, does it? We tend to keep people at a distance, preferring to interact with each other through projections or facades. What I mean is, we only let people see what we *want* them to see. This is one of the reasons why we love social media so much. We can carefully construct this image of ourselves that we broadcast to the world. I mean, how many of us are going to put an unflattering profile picture up, am I right?

Several years ago I received an award for being one of the top forty leaders under the age of forty in the city where I lived. I'm not sure why they were so into the number forty, but that's beside the point. Apparently it was a somewhat prestigious award, and I was really flattered to have been selected for it. All forty of us who were chosen received invitations to this big, fancy dinner downtown in order to "network." It was one of those dinners with a jazz band and that really great ice—you know, the kind with the hole in the middle of it. I remember walking in and immediately feeling completely out of my league. Just about everyone there had on designer clothes. I got my suit half-off at a department store, and I'm pretty sure there was a toothpaste stain on my tie. Most of the people I talked with had gone to Ivy League schools; I went to a Bible college none of them had heard of. This one guy was telling me how we was learning to fly a plane in his spare time, and it was right about then that I started to ask myself, "What am I doing here?" I didn't want anyone to know who I was or what I did. In fact, I was tempted to make up something else instead of telling them my true story. But instead, I just slowly made my way over to a nice dark corner and opted to be that "mysterious" guy for the rest of the night.

This is a little snapshot of how many of us live our lives. It's like we are afraid we are going to be found out—that if people discover who we really are, then they won't accept us. As a result, most of our relationships stay shallow; we can easily find ourselves surrounded by people and yet still feeling alone.

We are these walking, talking dichotomies. We long for community and connection, but we are broken versions of ourselves and so we hide from one of the things we have been wired for: each other. It's no wonder that one of the first signs of God's redemption taking a leap forward was this beautiful demonstration of community that we see in Acts 2 and 4. These former strangers from all over the world began opening up their homes and eating together with glad and sincere hearts, and that was evidence of God's kingdom.

So then, how do we follow their lead? How do we not only ensure that we are all on the same page (one mind), but that we are all opening our real selves to one another (one heart)? Now that we know what it means to be of one heart, let's begin to discuss what it takes on our part to experience it.

Romans 12:9-21 offers some key ways we can experience unity of heart. Of course, we could spend quite a while delving into all of the ways that a passage like this challenges the way we interact with one another. But in terms of being of one heart, this passage lifts up three Core Postures that allow us to connect with one anther at a deeper level: Vulnerability, Compassion, and Grace.

Vulnerability

That's a scary word, isn't it? To be vulnerable is to open ourselves up and allow ourselves to be seen. That is exactly what this passage calls us to do. It starts by saying that love must be sincere: "Love should be shown without pretending" (Romans 12:9). The Greek in this sentence literally means without hypocrisy. *Hypocrites* were play actors in the ancient world. They were people who would wear masks, change their voices, and take on a different persona in order to play a role. Essentially, they would pretend to be someone else.

We may not be into play-acting, but we all wear our masks. Our tendency is to try to seem stronger than we actually are, to seem as if we have it all together. But in order for our love to be sincere, the masks must come down.

My wife and I had this small leak under our kitchen sink for almost a year. I am not exactly a handyman, and I certainly don't know anything about plumbing. It wasn't a horrible leak, so at first we put a small glass bowl down to catch the water until we got it fixed. When the bowl would fill up it would smell awful—I mean portable-toilet awful—and we would empty out the water and then put the bowl back. My wife would ask me when I was going to get the leak fixed, and I would assure her that I would get to it soon.

After about ten months of dumping out stinky water, she decided to take care of the leak herself. One night she was out with some of her girlfriends, and she shared with them about our leaky sink and asked if they knew any good plumbers. They immediately all volunteered their husbands, assuring her that their husbands would be able to fix it for us. Of course, she thought that was great. When she got home she eagerly shared with me the good news. . . .

I reacted as if she had told them that I still sleep with my favorite childhood stuffed animal (which I don't do, by the way). In other words, I got really upset. I didn't want all of those people to know that I had no idea how to fix a leaky sink. Plus, once they did help I would have to deal with that nagging sense that I owed them one—that I was in the hole. The whole situation made me vulnerable: My limitations were exposed, and I was placing myself in someone's debt. I didn't like that.

If we admit it, we are all afraid of being vulnerable. Our fear of vulnerability has a lot to do with our culture's obsession with independence. In our minds, healthy, strong, successful people are those who don't need anyone else and who can take care of themselves. If we have to rely on someone else, we feel that we are lacking, that we are somehow *less.* This emphasis on independence cripples our relationships. For instance, how do you feel when you have to ask for help? How many apologies do you weave into the request? "I really hate to ask this of you . . . " or "I know this has to be such a bother, but . . . " At the same time, we tend to keep these mental scorecards of who has done what for us and what we have done for others. We struggle even to enjoy the gift of what someone else has done or wants to do for us because we suffocate it with a deep sense of obligation.

Instead of being vulnerable, we choose to wear our masks and hold onto our illusions of independence, and all the while the stench coming from under our sink is getting to be unbearable.

Jesus calls us away from our obsession with independence and invites us into communities of interdependence, in which we can let down the masks and allow ourselves to be truly seen.

It takes a decent amount of humility to admit that you need some help, or to ask someone for something. The last time I checked, the Scriptures are clear that humility is a good thing.

There's something I've noticed about vulnerability, particularly in small-group communities. Vulnerable is contagious. When someone is courageous enough to throw something out on the table—to share a struggle or admit a need—the other people in the group tend to follow suit. Believe it or not, we aren't as alone as we think we are.

Compassion

The second Core Posture is compassion. Compassion is the other side of vulnerability. If vulnerability means letting other people look into our lives, compassion means looking into theirs.

Paul lifts up the importance of compassion in Romans Chapter 12. In verse 15, he writes, "Be happy with those who are happy, and cry with those who are crying." So if someone is celebrating, celebrate with her. If someone is grieving a loss, grieve it along with him. The author implores us to be with one another, not just physically, but in every way possible.

This is what compassion is. We see exhortations to be compassionate throughout the New Testament letters. In Ephesians 4:32, Paul tells us to be kind and compassionate to one another. The author of Colossians 3:12 actually instructs us to clothe ourselves with compassion like a garment. In 1 Peter 3:8, the author calls us to be sympathetic, kind, and compassionate toward each other. The word *compassion* is one of the more colorful words in the Greek language. It means to feel something in your intestines or your guts. It makes perfect sense, really. When you hear of someone you care about going through a difficult time, where do you feel for them at? In your guts, right? You get a knot in your stomach or an ache in your heart. That's what compassion is. It is to feel what another person is feeling, and it has a powerful way of bringing us closer together.

My wife and I lived in this tiny, one-bedroom apartment when we first got married. The walls were paper-thin, and you could hear just about everything that was going on in the rooms around you. Our neighbor below us, let's call him Bud, had a dog that he kept locked up in his bathroom while he was away. The dog would bark the entire time Bud was gone. We would be lying in bed, and it would sound like the dog was in our bedroom.

One time Bud was gone overnight, and that dog barked from around 8:00 at night to around 10:00 the next morning. We decided to call management and let them know what was going on, and they told us that they would talk to him and take care of it. The next day we got a phone call from the apartment complex to give us an update. They told us that they had talked to Bud about locking the dog in the bathroom, but they said he was really angry that we had reported him. They advised us to try to steer clear of him. Of course, I was perfectly fine with him coming up to my apartment. We could deal with it ourselves, I thought. After all, we were the ones who had the right to be upset about everything. We were the ones losing sleep!

That Friday, around 10:30 at night, we heard a knock on our door. I jumped up hoping it was Bud. I had rehearsed what I was going to say and even freshened up on my Judo. That last part isn't true, but it makes the story more interesting. When I opened the door, I saw Bud; and immediately the smell of alcohol hit me like a ton of bricks. He was hammered. Something in me shifted when I looked at him standing in my doorway. I knew that he lived alone, and I remember looking at him and thinking, "Who gets this drunk on a Friday night, by themselves? What's his life like?" I honestly stood there, in the doorway of my apartment, and I felt sorry for the guy. When I heard the knock on my door, I was ready to let Bud have it, but as soon as I stepped out of my world and made an effort to understand his, all of that changed. Our interaction that night didn't lead to any sort of fight or argument. We actually stood out in the hallway and talked for a while, and then after that we were really friendly whenever we saw each other.

Compassion is about stepping into someone else's world, getting to know someone else's story. Doing that has a way of bringing us closer and helping us connect.

Chances are, there will be people in our small group communities that we don't exactly understand. They might even get under our skin and drive us nuts. How much do we know about them? What have they been through? What's it like to be them? Do we know what life was like for them growing up? Do we know what kind of situation they are living in now? What do they wish they could change about themselves? How do they feel they have grown over the past year? Getting to know some of these things and practicing a little compassion moves us all closer together.

Grace

All throughout Romans 12:9-21, the author encourages us to extend grace to one another. In verse 14, he says, "Bless people who harass you—bless and don't curse them." In verse 17, he tells us, "Don't pay back anyone for their evil actions with evil actions." The passage concludes in verses 19-20, saying, "Don't try to get revenge for yourselves, my dear friends, but leave room for God's wrath. It is written, *Revenge belongs to me; I will pay it back, says the Lord. Instead, If your enemy is hungry, feed him; if he is thirsty, give him a drink. By doing this, you will pile burning coals of fire upon his head. Don't be defeated by evil, but defeat evil with good.*" The imagery of hot coals on someone's head was a symbol of repentance. What the author means, then, is that the grace we extend to those who have wronged us may be the very thing that points them toward repentance.

If we are going to share our lives with one another in true community, grace must be like the air we breathe. Failures will happen. We are going to let one another down. We are going to hurt each other, sometimes intentionally and sometimes unintentionally. What will determine the depth and longevity of our relationships is not the absence of conflict, but how quickly and abundantly we extend grace, particularly in the form of forgiveness. Nothing separates people faster and more permanently than un-forgiveness.

Jesus takes un-forgiveness very seriously. In Matthew Chapter 5, Jesus says, "Therefore, if you bring your gift to the altar and there remember that your brother or sister has something against you, leave your gift at the altar and go. First make things right with your brother or sister and then come back and offer your gift" (Matthew 5:23-24). In a culture where everything centered on what happened at the altar, to say that something else was more important would have been pretty shocking. Jesus is saying that there is no point in seeking communion with God if there is an unresolved issue between you and someone else. This would be like Jesus saying, "Don't even bother going to church if you are going to drive there in silence because there are unresolved issues in the family."

At first, this may seem a bit extreme, but remember: We are made in the image of a relational God. This means that our relationships are a vital part of who we are, and nothing reveals the health of our connection with God more clearly than the condition of our relationships with one another. The author of First John says it like this: "If anyone says, I love God, and hates a brother or sister, he is a liar, because the person who doesn't love a brother or sister who can be seen can't love God, who can't be seen." (1 John 4:20).

This is why Jesus takes the issue of un-forgiveness so seriously. It is damaging to us in every way, and it absolutely destroys our relationships. No wonder the early church was so devoted to the Lord's Supper—to Communion. That meal brings us all to the table of God's boundless grace offered to us in Jesus Christ. Often when there is some sort of conflict in our community, there is nothing better for us to do than gather around the bread and the cup in order to be reminded and empowered by God's forgiveness for us, so that we may somehow extend it toward one another.

It will be important to discuss what a commitment to grace will look like in your small group community, but one of the most effective ways for it to be implemented is through prayer. Prayer is another one of the practices to which the early church was devoted. Not only does it tap into God's power to change what is around us, but prayer also has the power to change what is in us—to soften our hearts toward one another. To pray for those we are at odds with by name is one of the ways we can allow God's grace to dissolve resentment and bitterness, moving us toward forgiveness and reconciliation.

So What/What's Next?

Being of one heart requires vulnerability, compassion, and grace. Through the rest of your time with ONE, you will be asked to incorporate what we have discussed in this session in a couple of ways.

1. Develop Ground Rules

We all don't play by the same rules. What I mean is, we all have different ways of doing things, different values, and different pet peeves. Often what causes most of the conflict in a group is some sort of misunderstanding of one another's rules. For instance, someone in your group may feel that being late is really offensive and disrespectful. They may value punctuality in themselves and expect it of others as a basic courtesy. There may be in this same group someone who is perpetually late, not because they are trying to be offensive, but because they have several children and getting out the door on time is no small task. If this goes on long enough, eventually the first person will begin to hold a grudge against the second person for failing to adhere to a rule that he didn't even know about.

It is essential to practice grace in all of this and assume the best about someone who is offending you. It is also important, however, for the group to develop a new set of rules. For instance, if this situation arises in your group, you will need to determine how you will deal with someone being late on a regular basis. Or what will you do when someone misses several sessions? Alternatively, what sort of language will your group use (or avoid) when things get real? I know of a small group who has prohibited accusatory language. They leave room for the source of the conflict to be a simple misunderstanding and use language such as, "I think" or "I feel." During the second four weeks of ONE, your group will participate in some activities that will help you establish some ground rules.

2. Share Your Story

Once your group is finished with ONE and meeting on your own, everyone will be asked to share their story. This is a way for you to practice both vulnerability and compassion. Don't feel like you have to share everything about your life at once; the depth of community you are working toward takes time and a certain level of trust. Sharing your stories at the outset, however, will help you all have some sense of where everyone is coming from.

Finally, let's add another word about the three questions: What are you grateful for? What are you anxious about? What are you learning? These three questions can serve as helpful tools to move us past skin-deep relationships. Sometimes in small group settings, we can hide behind curriculums and studies in order to avoid talking about what is actually going on in our lives. Studies can be a great resource for a group, but not if we use them as a decoy. If we stay committed to wrestling with these questions through the week and then answering them when we are together, they can help us maintain unity of heart and mind.

The gospel challenges us to a deeper level of intimacy with one another. This will not always be easy and it is guaranteed to be uncomfortable at times, but I can promise you that it will be worth it. Life is an incredible gift, and like most gifts it is better when it is shared.

IN YOUR GROUP

The Three Questions

As you meet in week three of your ONE experience, take note of the way relationships have begun to grow and develop in the group. Be encouraged by this and make a choice once again to invest in this time together by being vulnerable with one another. Before you begin this week's study, as a group, take time to answer the second of the three questions.

1. What are you grateful for?

2. What are you anxious about?

3. What are you learning?

Study the Scriptures

Read Acts 2:42-47 and Acts 4:32-37 on the following pages. Make notes on the questions below in the space provided there.

1. What are some of your most prized possessions? If your house were burning down, what would you save and why?

2. Acts 4:32 says, the community of believers "was one in heart and mind." What does oneness of heart mean to you?

3. What word, phrase, or verse in these passages best demonstrates the group's oneness of heart?

Acts 2:42-47

[42]The believers devoted themselves to the apostles' teaching, to the community, to their shared meals, and to their prayers. [43]A sense of awe came over everyone. God performed many wonders and signs through the apostles. [44]All the believers were united and shared everything. [45]They would sell pieces of property and possessions and distribute the proceeds to everyone who needed them. [46]Every day, they met together in the temple and ate in their homes. They shared food with gladness and simplicity. [47]They praised God and demonstrated God's goodness to everyone. The Lord added daily to the community those who were being saved.

Acts 4:32-37

[32]The community of believers was one in heart and mind. None of them would say, "This is mine!" about any of their possessions, but held everything in common. [33]The apostles continued to bear powerful witness to the resurrection of the Lord Jesus, and an abundance of grace was at work among them all. [34]There were no needy persons among them. Those who owned properties or houses would sell them, bring the proceeds from the sales, [35]and place them in the care and under the authority of the apostles. Then it was distributed to anyone who was in need.

[36]Joseph, whom the apostles nicknamed Barnabas (that is, "one who encourages"), was a Levite from Cyprus. [37]He owned a field, sold it, brought the money, and placed it in the care and under the authority of the apostles.

Experiencing God Together

Read Romans 12:9-21 below. Answer the question on the next page in the space provided.

Romans 12:9-21

[9]Love should be shown without pretending. Hate evil, and hold on to what is good. [10]Love each other like the members of your family. Be the best at showing honor to each other. [11]Don't hesitate to be enthusiastic—be on fire in the Spirit as you serve the Lord! [12]Be happy in your hope, stand your ground when you're in trouble, and devote yourselves to prayer. [13]Contribute to the needs of God's people, and welcome strangers into your home. [14]Bless people who harass you—bless and don't curse them. [15]Be happy with those who are happy, and cry with those who are crying. [16]Consider everyone as equal, and don't think that you're better than anyone else. Instead, associate with people who have no status. Don't think that you're so smart. [17]Don't pay back anyone for their evil actions with evil actions, but show respect for what everyone else believes is good.

[18]If possible, to the best of your ability, live at peace with all people. [19]Don't try to get revenge for yourselves, my dear friends, but leave room for God's wrath. It is written, *Revenge belongs to me; I will pay it back, says the Lord.* [20]*Instead, If your enemy is hungry, feed him; if he is thirsty, give him a drink. By doing this, you will pile burning coals of fire upon his head.* [21]Don't be defeated by evil, but defeat evil with good.

This passage has a lot to say about what our love for one another ought to look like. What specific wisdom does it offer us in terms of the posture that is required of us in order to be of one heart?

Vulnerability, Compassion, and Grace

Draw or write your responses to the questions below.

1. When have you experienced vulnerability, either opening up to someone or having someone else open up to you?

2. What can the group do to encourage vulnerability, to make the group a safe space for people to open up and truly share themselves with one another?

3. How can the group create a culture of compassion and grace toward one another? What practices can you implement to help these postures take root among you as individuals and within the group as a whole?

ONE CHALLENGE

Arrange another one-on-one meeting with a fellow group member this week, preferably a different member than the one you met with in week one. Spend some time getting to know each other a little better, starting with generalities and letting the conversation become more organic as you go. You might discuss hobbies, family background, work life, or anything else that interests you. Try to practice vulnerability, compassion, and grace in this discussion. Step out of your comfort zone a little bit and share something with the other person that you normally might not share with someone you're just getting to know. Listen to the other person with compassion and grace. Be sure that you respect the other person's trust and maintain confidentiality if you are asked to do so. Commit to praying for each other throughout the week.

I'm meeting with:_____

DEVOTIONAL

What are you learning?

Psalm 19 tells us that the heavens declare the glory of God (Psalm 19:1). The word for glory is the Hebrew word *kavod*. The root of the word means heavy or weighty, and because of that it can mean something substantial and valuable. Something that has glory is something of importance or significance—it's something that matters.

You know the glory of God. It's that thing that you experience in those moments when you realize that there is way more going on than what you had previously thought. Experiencing the glory of God is what happens when we become aware of the bigger meaning behind it all—when we lean in, pay attention, and recognize how beautiful it all is.

According to the author of Psalm 19, this glory is not located in select places and times, but is everywhere, all around us all of the time. If we believe this to be true, then every day presents itself with an opportunity to learn something new about God, about ourselves, and about the world we live in. The real question is, are we paying attention? Are we actively looking for God's glory?

The point of following Jesus is to do just that: to take on his way of life and learn from him what it means to be a true, genuine human being. The hope we have in Jesus is not just the forgiveness of sin but also freedom from sin and nothing less than total transformation.

That's what this question, "What are you learning?" is all about. It's about looking for an opportunity to learn something new in any and all situations, developing a habit of pursuing the full life of God.

Day 1

Read Psalm 19

If God's glory is everywhere, why aren't we more aware of it? What can we learn from this psalm about becoming more aware of God's presence? How does it ready us to answer the question, "What are you learning?"

Day 2

Read Colossians 3:1-17

The foundation for the growth that matters is faith in Jesus Christ, and it is from that faith that we receive our true identity. What does this passage have to say about finding our identity in Jesus Christ? What does it mean to set our hearts on things above? What in your life would change if you were to become more committed to those things?

Day 3

Read Luke 18:1-8

What do you think is the point of this parable? Have you in anyway grown complacent or stagnant in your faith? Explain. What can you do to reawaken your passion or to push yourself further?

Day 4

Read Psalm 95

How did the people harden their hearts toward God when they were wandering in the wilderness? Is there some sense of conviction that you have been trying to tune out? What would it look like for you to respond to God's voice?

Day 5

Read Proverbs 1:1-33

What does it mean when it says that "wisdom begins with the fear of the Lᴏʀᴅ"? What sort of fear does it mean, and why would that be the beginning of wisdom? In what ways are you seeking wisdom?

Day 6

Read 2 Peter 1:3-11

How does this passage challenge us to grow in our faith? What does it mean to "share the divine nature"? Which one of the eight virtues in verses 5-7 are you the most uncomfortable with? Why? What is something that you can commit to this year that will take you out of your comfort zone and help grow you forward?

Day 7

Read Matthew 19:13-30

What does Jesus mean when he says that the kingdom of heaven belongs to people like the children? What do children have to teach us about how to live life well? How do you relate to the rich man? What sorts of distractions keep you away from what you need most?

———

Session 4:

ONE WAY

G ood news is impossible to keep to yourself, isn't it? C. S. Lewis once said, "We delight to praise what we enjoy because the praise not merely expresses but completes the enjoyment; it is its appointed consummation" (From *Reflections on the Psalms: The Celebrated Musings on One of the Most Intriguing Books of the Bible*; Harcourt, 1958; page 95).

Appointed consummation. Essentially there is a joy we experience when we share something that has moved us. It's like when you hear a great joke or when you hear a new favorite song; what is your first impulse? To find someone to share it with, right? This is why one of the first things a couple does right after they become engaged is to pull out their phones and tell as many people as possible. That's the nature of good news. It has to get out; it begs us to share it.

This is certainly true of the gospel—the good news—of Jesus Christ. It's one of the main themes of the Book of Acts—the explosive inside-out growth of the early church. Jesus told the disciples that they would be his witnesses in Jerusalem, Judea, Samaria, and to the ends of the earth; and that is exactly what happened. Not only was the early church united in mind and heart, but they were committed to heading one way: outward. That's because the gospel is the kind of news that can't keep quite or stay to itself. It has been changing people's lives and flipping the world right-side up for more than two thousand years, but its not done yet. . . .

In Acts Chapter 1, Jesus has just been raised from the dead, and he is teaching his disciples about what? He's teaching about the Kingdom—the rule or reign—of God (Acts 1:3). The disciples were struggling to wrap their brains around everything that had just happened, so they asked Jesus, "Lord, are you going to restore the kingdom to Israel now?" (verse 6). This is a lot like the dreaded road trip question parents hear, "Are we there yet?"

We tend to give the disciples a hard time for their lack of understanding, but think about how strange all of this must have seemed to them. Sure, they believed that Jesus was the Messiah, but they didn't see crucifixion and resurrection coming as part of the deal. No one expected the Messiah to be crucified, but three days later he was eating lunch with them. The shock of that reversal must have still been in their minds while Jesus was teaching them at the beginning of Acts.

But the fact is, the disciples were mistaken when they asked if Jesus was about to "restore the kingdom to Israel" (Acts 1:6). The disciples weren't thinking big enough. They thought that the promises of God only involved the people of Israel and that the Messiah was going to rescue them from their political enemies, namely the Roman Empire. Jesus sidestepped their question, and instead of answering it directly, he pointed them to something bigger. Jesus said to them, "It isn't for you to know the times or seasons that the Father has set by his own authority. Rather, you will receive power when the Holy Spirit has come upon you, and you will be my witnesses in Jerusalem, in all Judea and Samaria, and to the end of the earth" (Acts 1:7-8). So even though he wasn't going to be with them physically, he was going to send his own Spirit that would reside in each of them, giving them the power to change everything. Two thousand years later, we are still living in the wake of what happened with that handful of scared cultural rejects who had trouble seeing the big picture at first.

Here in Acts Chapter 1, Jesus was giving them their mission statement. They were to be his witnesses, first in Jerusalem, where they were at the time, and then in the two surrounding areas, Judea and Samaria. In other words, this kingdom of God movement, which was then confined in Jerusalem, wasn't going to stay put; it was going to move out from there and eventually reach all the way "to the ends of the earth" (Acts 1:8).

This is exactly what you find happening as you read through the Book of Acts. A pattern develops. The church experiences opposition and persecution, which forces it to scatter. But instead of shrinking back and retreating inward, the church continues to move outward and ventures into new territories. By Chapter 17, Paul is sharing the gospel in the city of Athens—the ancient capital of the Greek Empire and an important center of religious and philosophical thought. When the book comes to a close in Chapter 28, Paul is in Rome, proclaiming the good news of Jesus Christ in the most important and powerful city in the world.

This pattern demonstrates the inside-out nature of God's kingdom. The kingdom of God is outwardly oriented. It's in its nature to grow and expand, and as it does so, it crosses over all of the lines the world uses to divide itself up.

This is evident right from the beginning with the disciple's mission statement. Jesus tells them they will be his witnesses in Jerusalem and then in Judea and Samaria (Acts 1:8). These weren't groups of people that were typically mentioned in the same sentence in the first century. The hatred between these two groups of people had been burning for many, many years. The parable of the Good Samaritan packs such a punch precisely because the Jews had such a low view of the people from Samaria (see Luke 10:25-37). The animosity went way back and had a long backstory, which we don't need to discuss for our purposes. The bottom line is the people of Judea and Samaria couldn't stand each other, and Jesus tells the disciples that they are to share the gospel with both of them. Yikes.

The church doesn't get moving until Acts Chapter 8, when a persecution breaks out at the hands of a young zealous Pharisee by the name of Saul. As a result, the church scatters and immediately begins to jump over dividing lines. In Acts 8, a disciple named Philip begins preaching the gospel in Samaria, where people believe his words and eventually receive the Holy Spirit (Acts 8:4-17). Later in the same chapter, the Spirit leads Philip to an Ethiopian man who hears the gospel, requests baptism, and receives the Holy Spirit (Acts 8:26-40). In this event, a racial barrier was crossed. No longer were the promises of God just for the Jewish people, but the good news was for everyone, no matter their ethnicity.

In Acts Chapter 9, that zealous young Pharisee named Saul encounters the resurrected Christ, comes to believe the gospel, and eventually receives the commission to share the good news with the Gentiles, the non-Jews. We know him by the name of Paul, and he became one of the most important messengers of Christianity and the author of much of the New Testament. With Paul's conversion, a religious line was crossed and a former enemy was welcomed in.

The outward expansion continues. In Chapter 10, a centurion in the Roman military by the name of Cornelius hears the gospel from Peter and receives the Holy Spirit. A political line has been crossed; now a Roman, one of the Jews' oppressors, is a part of the kingdom of God.

When you step back and look at the Acts from a big picture perspective, it is jaw-dropping. It begins in Chapter 1 with the disciples still thinking that God is only concerned with their people, the Jews. But by the time the book ends in Chapter 28, Paul, a former enemy, is sharing openly about the kingdom of God in Rome, the capital city of the very empire that stands in opposition to it.

Talk about inside-out! The kingdom of God is a kingdom that moves in one direction—outward. This is a movement that advances, not with its arms crossed but with them wide-open, ready, and eager to welcome those who are currently on the outside.

On the Outside Looking In

I remember when my son was invited to his very first birthday party. He was really excited; the kid loves to be around his friends just like his daddy. About an hour or so into the party I noticed him inside playing with some toys by himself. This seemed a bit odd, so I went over to investigate. In his two-year-old way he tried to explain to me that the big boys told him he was too little to play with them outside. He was a good deal younger than the rest of the kids, and I knew it wasn't anything malicious, but as I watched my son play by himself I was heartbroken. At this birthday party he was really looking forward to, he felt left out. The situation gave me flashbacks of all the times in my life I felt like I was on the outside looking in. Do you have any of those?

You may have grown up going to the local skating rink. When I was a kid, it seemed like every birthday party was held at the skating rink. I actually loved to skate because it was the only time I was fast. As much as I loved being at the skating rink, though, there was a time when I didn't want to be there: couple's skate. I didn't have a whole lot of self-confidence back then, so I was the kid who had to skate off the floor and watch all the happy preteen couples skate to the newest Boyz-II-Men song. I don't share that with you to make you feel sorry for me. (Don't worry; I make my wife go to the skating rink with me all the time. Not really, but it's a good ending to the story!) I share this with you because I'm certain you've had moments like that too. At one time or another, we've all felt like we have been on the outside looking in.

Whether it was the lunchroom in middle school and high school or maybe even the place where we work now, we know what it feels like to be excluded, to be on the outside. This is the world we live in; it is relentlessly exclusive. It's all about drawing lines, picking sides, us versus them. It's a world divided up into overly simplistic categories and sweeping generalizations: These people are the good guys, and those people are the bad guys. This group is the problem, and that group is the solution. Those are the ones who need to be saved, and these are the ones who should do the saving. How often do we hear or think something along the lines of, "Well what did you expect, they are all like that," or "That's just how people from there do things"?

We all know what it feels like to be excluded. We have all felt judged, pushed off to the side, categorized, or labeled. At the same time, we have all at some time or another participated in making someone else feel this way too. But the good news is that Jesus came to rescue us from all of this—to tear down the walls and blur the lines that the world uses to separate and divide—and to bring us into a unified kingdom of God. As Galatians 3:28 says, "There is neither Jew nor Greek; there is neither slave nor free; nor is there male and female, for you are all one in Christ Jesus."

One of the places where we get to model this unified kingdom is in our small-group communities, and we can do that in two ways: multiplication and mission.

Multiplication

That last line of Acts 2:42-47 is something else. "The Lord added daily to the community those who were being saved." Wouldn't it be exciting to be a part of something that contagious? This is what happens when a group of people take Jesus' call to love one another seriously. People on the outside want in.

There is a quote that is often credited to several different people, so it's hard to place the original source. But whoever said it, it is profoundly true. It goes something like this: "The church is the only organization that exists primarily for its non-members." Jesus reveals to us a God who will leave the ninety-nine sheep in order to find one that is lost. As his church, we are called to embody this sort of passion for those who do not know the saving love of God for themselves. One of the ways we do that in our small groups is through multiplication.

In Acts Chapter 8, when the persecution breaks out, it says in verse 1 that all except the apostles were scattered throughout Judea and Samaria. Then in verse 4 it says that those who had been scattered preached the Word wherever they went. Remember the apostles—the leadership—stayed in Jerusalem, while everyone else scattered. What that means is, the "professionals" aren't the ones preaching the Word. Imagine that! This is why the early church grew at such a remarkable rate. Everyone bought in, everyone took it personally, and everyone knew they had a role to play. Proclaiming the good news of Jesus Christ was everyone's calling.

This is where the practice of multiplication comes in. It's one thing to add new people to your group, and that can be a good thing up to a point. But imagine a network of small groups that was committed to identifying and sending out people to start new groups, which consisted of people in their various circles who are on the outside looking in? That's got "movement" written all over it.

In our day and age people are hungry for authentic relationships and honest community. This is true for those who identify as religious and for those who don't. For many people, their entry into God's kingdom won't happen by stepping foot into a sanctuary, but by stepping foot into someone's living room.

I remember being sent out to start a small group when I was in my early twenties. It was made up of people who were relatively new to the Christian faith. There was one guy in the group—we will call him Larry the Ladies' Man—who was only there because his roommate had volunteered their apartment for us to meet in. Larry was an interesting guy. He was twenty-three and recently divorced, and his ex-wife was living with another man. You can imagine how hard this would be for anyone, but especially for a twenty-three-year old.

Larry's way of dealing with his divorce was promiscuity. He made an effort to hook up with as many women as he possibly could, and at this time in his life he wasn't sure how he felt about God, or Jesus, or faith in general. And yet for some reason he chose to participate in the group.

We had been meeting for a few weeks when the season of Lent rolled around, and we all decided to give something up for the forty days of Lent. We were all pretty surprised to hear Larry say that he was going to refrain from randomly hooking up with girls for seven weeks. That just gives you an idea of where he was when we first started meeting together.

You know, no one in the group ever pointed a finger at Larry; we didn't constantly tell him that he was wrong. We did, however, ask him a lot of questions, and we tried to point him towards something better. We certainly talked about Jesus a lot, and we shared what he was doing in our own lives. As our group continued to grow, it was amazing to watch a change take place in Larry's life. After several months of meeting together, he became the guy who would call someone out if they made an inappropriate joke about a female. I remember the first night he did it, we were all sort of caught off guard. I mean this was coming from the same guy who gave up being promiscuous for Lent! Now, Larry is married to an amazing woman and is actually leading worship at his church.

Through multiplication we can empower and send one another out to create new outposts for the Kingdom where people on the outside can feel like they belong before they have their beliefs straightened out all the way.

In the second half of this course, you and your group will discuss how and when you will multiply yourselves. This isn't something you ought to rush into. It isn't a good idea for a group to multiply in under a year. There are some important conversations to have and action steps that will need to be put in place before your group will be ready. Right now, more than anything it is important to begin your journey together knowing that is something you are aiming for.

Mission

Not only do we embody the inside-out nature of the kingdom through multiplication, but we do so through mission as well.

We already pointed out that the early church enjoyed the favor, or the respect, of all the people in Jerusalem, but it's worth revisiting. It didn't matter if you were a part of the group or not, you were glad the church was in Jerusalem because they made the city a better place.

What happens inside our community must impact the world outside of our community.

This has always been Jesus' intention for his church. Matthew 16 is the first time the idea of the church is mentioned in any of the Gospels. Jesus and his disciples had traveled to the area of Caesarea Philippi, and it is here that Jesus asked his disciples, "Who do people say the Human One is?" (Matthew 16:13). They responded, "Some say John the Baptist, others Elijah, and still others Jeremiah or one of the prophets" (verse 14). Jesus then made the question personal, asking them, "And what about you? Who do you say I am?" (verse 15). This is a question that each of us have to answer as well. Who do we say Jesus is? Peter answers the question correctly, declaring that Jesus is in fact the Messiah, the Christ (verse 16). Of course, based on what happens later in the passage, Peter is mistaken about what Jesus' messianic identity means. Peter thought that Jesus was headed to the throne in the palace, but Jesus was headed to the cross on the hill, and he invites all of us to do the same thing as well (see Matthew 16:21-23).

Jesus affirms Peter for answering the question correctly, and then in verse 18 he says, "I tell you that you are Peter. And I'll build my church on this rock [In Greek *Peter* means rock or stone]. The gates of the underworld won't be able to stand against it."

It's interesting that Jesus chose Caesarea Philippi to ask the disciples this question and to make this statement about his church. Jesus didn't just happen to be in Caesarea Philippi. Caesarea Philippi is located in the very northern part of Israel, and during the time of Jesus it was a center of pagan worship. The city was famous for a giant rock and at the base of a rock was a large cave, or a crack, that the people referred to as the gates of Hades, or the underworld. All around this crack there were temples dedicated to pagan gods. So when Jesus says to Peter, "I'll build my church on this rock" and "the gates of the underworld won't be able to stand against it," he is saying something about the role Peter will play in leading the church. And at the same time, Jesus is making a statement about the role of his church in the world.

Jesus envisioned his church reaching out to a lost and broken world, not retreating from it. We tend to identify ourselves as Christian based on the amount of distance we can keep between the world and ourselves, but where is Jesus going to build his church? Right in the middle of the world in all its mess. In the very city where pagan worship is so prominent, Jesus wants to start a movement of people who are committed to a different way. Just a few verses later Jesus says, "Then Jesus said to his disciples, 'All who want to come after me must say no to themselves, take up their cross, and follow me. All who want to save their lives will lose them. But all who lose their lives because of me will find them'" (Matthew 16:24-25). Jesus expects the people of his church to take up their cross and follow him into the broken places of the world, in order to partner with him in putting the pieces back together.

This is where true life is found. First John tells us that God is love, and in Chapter 3 the author says, "This is how we know love: Jesus laid down his life for us" (1 John 3:16). God doesn't just arbitrarily call us to serve and to give of ourselves simply because he wants to rain on our parade. God calls us to live this way because that is what he is like—outwardly oriented. Sacrificial, self-giving love is the very essence of who God is, and orienting ourselves in this way leads to the best kind of life. This is what Jesus means by his words in Matthew 16:24-25. "Come follow me; let me show you who you really are. You want to experience real life? Then you have to give yourself away."

Typically in a church, the mission is carried out by a handful of people and the rest see themselves as a part of it by association. Sitting in the seat on Sunday mornings and putting money in the offering plate makes one a part of what this church is doing. Such is the usual mindset. Yet if we think in this way, we are missing out on so much, because the joy comes from rolling up your sleeves and getting your hands dirty.

Imagine a network of small-group communities where the people were encouraging one another as individuals to live out of their unique call from God and at the same time they were committed to a collective mission as well. Picture a church where one small group has adopted a third grade class at an "at-risk" school in the area, where another small group is investing in young girls who have been rescued from sex trafficking, and where a third group is facilitating a community garden in a part of town where people struggle to afford fresh fruits and vegetables. Sign me up for one of those small groups, because they are the kind of outwardly oriented life that reflects God's very self.

During the second half of this course, you and your group will be encouraged to begin discussing what your common mission will be. How are you going to serve together? What sort of broken place in your community are you going to pour yourselves into? Not only will this serve to advance the Kingdom, but it will bring you closer together as well.

This concludes the first half of our time together. For the next four weeks, we will work to implement what we have learned by creating a covenant statement involving the three Core Practices, develop ground rules that reflect the three Core Postures, and share and interact with one another's life stories. From here on out you are the stars of the show. You know what you need to know; now it's time to talk about how you will put it into practice.

These next four weeks can be extremely valuable for you and your group, but it will require you to participate. So do yourself and all your group members a favor. Fully engage, be honest, and don't offer or accept pat answers.

The next set of devotionals will take you back to review some of the things we talked about over the past several weeks and prepare you for your time with the group.

Spend some time in prayer as a group, and ask God to prepare your hearts and your minds to fully embrace your shared life together and begin the journey toward becoming one.

IN YOUR GROUP

The Three Questions

Before you dive into this week's study, start with some intentional time talking about your spiritual life over the past week. Take time for each person in the group to answer the third of the Three Questions:

1. What are you grateful for?

2. What are you anxious about?

3. **What are you learning?**

Study the Scriptures

Read the Scripture passages on the following pages. How do you see the inside-out nature of the kingdom of God demonstrated in them? Write or draw your responses in the space provided after each passage.

Acts 1:1-9

[1]Theophilus, the first scroll I wrote concerned everything Jesus did and taught from the beginning, [2]right up to the day when he was taken up into heaven. Before he was taken up, working in the power of the Holy Spirit, Jesus instructed the apostles he had chosen. [3]After his suffering, he showed them that he was alive with many convincing proofs. He appeared to them over a period of forty days, speaking to them about God's kingdom. [4]While they were eating together, he ordered them not to leave Jerusalem but to wait for what the Father had promised. He said, "This is what you heard from me: [5]John baptized with water, but in only a few days you will be baptized with the Holy Spirit." [6]As a result, those who had gathered together asked Jesus, "Lord, are you going to restore the kingdom to Israel now?" [7]Jesus replied, "It isn't for you to know the times or seasons that the Father has set by his own authority. [8]Rather, you will receive power when the Holy Spirit has come upon you, and you will be my witnesses in Jerusalem, in all Judea and Samaria, and to the end of the earth." [9]After Jesus said these things, as they were watching, he was lifted up and a cloud took him out of their sight.

Acts 8:1-8; 26-35

8 [1]Saul was in full agreement with Stephen's murder.

The church scatters

At that time, the church in Jerusalem began to be subjected to vicious harassment. Everyone except the apostles was scattered throughout the regions of Judea and Samaria. [2]Some pious men buried Stephen and deeply grieved over him. [3]Saul began to wreak havoc against the church. Entering one house after another, he would drag off both men and women and throw them into prison.

Philip in Samaria

[4]Those who had been scattered moved on, preaching the good news along the way. [5]Philip went down to a city in Samaria and began to preach Christ to them. [6]The crowds were united by what they heard Philip say and the signs they saw him perform, and they gave him their undivided attention. [7]With loud shrieks, unclean spirits came out of many people, and many who were paralyzed or crippled were healed. [8]There was great rejoicing in that city.

Philip and the Ethiopian eunuch

[26]An angel from the Lord spoke to Philip, "At noon, take the road that leads from Jerusalem to Gaza." (This is a desert road.) [27]So he did. Meanwhile, an Ethiopian man was on his way home from Jerusalem, where he had come to worship. He was a eunuch and an official responsible for the entire treasury of Candace. (Candace is the title given to the Ethiopian queen.) [28]He was reading the prophet Isaiah while sitting in his carriage. [29]The Spirit told Philip, "Approach this carriage and stay with it."

[30]Running up to the carriage, Philip heard the man reading the prophet Isaiah. He asked, "Do you really understand what you are reading?"

[31]The man replied, "Without someone to guide me, how could I?" Then he invited Philip to climb up and sit with him. [32]This was the passage of scripture he was reading:

Like a sheep he was led to the slaughter
   and like a lamb before its shearer is silent
   so he didn't open his mouth.

³³*In his humiliation justice was taken away from him.*
Who can tell the story of his descendants
   because his life was taken from the earth?

³⁴The eunuch asked Philip, "Tell me, about whom does the prophet say this? Is he talking about himself or someone else?" ³⁵Starting with that passage, Philip proclaimed the good news about Jesus to him.

Acts 9:1-19

9 [1]Meanwhile, Saul was still spewing out murderous threats against the Lord's disciples. He went to the high priest, [2]seeking letters to the synagogues in Damascus. If he found persons who belonged to the Way, whether men or women, these letters would authorize him to take them as prisoners to Jerusalem. [3]During the journey, as he approached Damascus, suddenly a light from heaven encircled him. [4]He fell to the ground and heard a voice asking him, "Saul, Saul, why are you harassing me?"

[5]Saul asked, "Who are you, Lord?"

"I am Jesus, whom you are harassing," came the reply. [6]"Now get up and enter the city. You will be told what you must do."

[7]Those traveling with him stood there speechless; they heard the voice but saw no one. [8]After they picked Saul up from the ground, he opened his eyes but he couldn't see. So they led him by the hand into Damascus. [9]For three days he was blind and neither ate nor drank anything.

[10]In Damascus there was a certain disciple named Ananias. The Lord spoke to him in a vision, "Ananias!"

He answered, "Yes, Lord."

[11]The Lord instructed him, "Go to Judas' house on Straight Street and ask for a man from Tarsus named Saul. He is praying. [12]In a vision he has seen a man named Ananias enter and put his hands on him to restore his sight."

[13]Ananias countered, "Lord, I have heard many reports about this man. People say he has done horrible things to your holy people in Jerusalem. [14]He's here with authority from the chief priests to arrest everyone who calls on your name."

[15]The Lord replied, "Go! This man is the agent I have chosen to carry my name before Gentiles, kings, and Israelites. [16]I will show him how much he must suffer for the sake of my name."

[17]Ananias went to the house. He placed his hands on Saul and said, "Brother Saul, the Lord sent me—Jesus, who appeared to you

on the way as you were coming here. He sent me so that you could see again and be filled with the Holy Spirit." [18]Instantly, flakes fell from Saul's eyes and he could see again. He got up and was baptized. [19]After eating, he regained his strength.

He stayed with the disciples in Damascus for several days.

Acts 10:1-35

Peter, Cornelius, and the Gentiles

10 ¹There was a man in Caesarea named Cornelius, a centurion in the Italian Company. ²He and his whole household were pious, Gentile God-worshippers. He gave generously to those in need among the Jewish people and prayed to God constantly. ³One day at nearly three o'clock in the afternoon, he clearly saw an angel from God in a vision. The angel came to him and said, "Cornelius!"

⁴Startled, he stared at the angel and replied, "What is it, Lord?"

The angel said, "Your prayers and your compassionate acts are like a memorial offering to God. ⁵Send messengers to Joppa at once and summon a certain Simon, the one known as Peter. ⁶He is a guest of Simon the tanner, whose house is near the seacoast." ⁷When the angel who was speaking to him had gone, Cornelius summoned two of his household servants along with a pious soldier from his personal staff. ⁸He explained everything to them, then sent them to Joppa.

⁹At noon on the following day, as their journey brought them close to the city, Peter went up on the roof to pray. ¹⁰He became hungry and wanted to eat. While others were preparing the meal, he had a visionary experience. ¹¹He saw heaven opened up and something like a large linen sheet being lowered to the earth by its four corners. ¹²Inside the sheet were all kinds of four-legged animals, reptiles, and wild birds. ¹³A voice told him, "Get up, Peter! Kill and eat!"

¹⁴Peter exclaimed, "Absolutely not, Lord! I have never eaten anything impure or unclean."

¹⁵The voice spoke a second time, "Never consider unclean what God has made pure." ¹⁶This happened three times, then the object was suddenly pulled back into heaven.

¹⁷Peter was bewildered about the meaning of the vision. Just then, the messengers sent by Cornelius discovered the whereabouts of Simon's house and arrived at the gate. ¹⁸Calling out, they inquired whether the Simon known as Peter was a guest there.

¹⁹While Peter was brooding over the vision, the Spirit interrupted him, "Look! Three people are looking for you. ²⁰Go downstairs. Don't ask questions; just go with them because I have sent them."

²¹So Peter went downstairs and told them, "I'm the one you are looking for. Why have you come?"

²²They replied, "We've come on behalf of Cornelius, a centurion and righteous man, a God-worshipper who is well-respected by all Jewish people. A holy angel directed him to summon you to his house and to hear what you have to say." ²³Peter invited them into the house as his guests.

The next day he got up and went with them, together with some of the believers from Joppa. ²⁴They arrived in Caesarea the following day. Anticipating their arrival, Cornelius had gathered his relatives and close friends. ²⁵As Peter entered the house, Cornelius met him and fell at his feet in order to honor him. ²⁶But Peter lifted him up, saying, "Get up! Like you, I'm just a human." ²⁷As they continued to talk, Peter went inside and found a large gathering of people. ²⁸He said to them, "You all realize that it is forbidden for a Jew to associate or visit with outsiders. However, God has shown me that I should never call a person impure or unclean. ²⁹For this reason, when you sent for me, I came without objection. I want to know, then, why you sent for me."

³⁰Cornelius answered, "Four days ago at this same time, three o'clock in the afternoon, I was praying at home. Suddenly a man in radiant clothing stood before me. ³¹He said, 'Cornelius, God has heard your prayers, and your compassionate acts are like a memorial offering to him. ³²Therefore, send someone to Joppa and summon Simon, who is known as Peter. He is a guest in the home of Simon the tanner, located near the seacoast.' ³³I sent for you right away, and you were kind enough to come. Now, here we are, gathered in the presence of God to listen to everything the Lord has directed you to say."

³⁴Peter said, "I really am learning that God doesn't show partiality to one group of people over another. ³⁵Rather, in every nation, whoever worships him and does what is right is acceptable to him.

On the Outside Looking In

Draw or write your responses to the questions provided below.

1. When have you felt like you've been left out? Why does it feel so painful to be on the outside looking in?

2. How does the way of the world differ from the kingdom of God?

3. What possibilities do you see for reaching out to those who are on the outside of your group or outside of the church?

Multiplication and Mission

Read Acts 2:42-47 and Acts 4:32-37. Consider the questions below and make notes about your responses in the space provided.

1. Where do you see evidence of multiplication in these passages?

2. Where do you see evidence of mission in these passages?

3. How can your small-group community demonstrate the inside-out nature of the gospel that we see described in these passages?

Acts 2:42-47

42The believers devoted themselves to the apostles' teaching, to the community, to their shared meals, and to their prayers. 43A sense of awe came over everyone. God performed many wonders and signs through the apostles. 44All the believers were united and shared everything. 45 They would sell pieces of property and possessions and distribute the proceeds to everyone who needed them. 46Every day, they met together in the temple and ate in their homes. They shared food with gladness and simplicity. 47They praised God and demonstrated God's goodness to everyone. The Lord added daily to the community those who were being saved.

Acts 4:32-37

[32]The community of believers was one in heart and mind. None of them would say, "This is mine!" about any of their possessions, but held everything in common. [33]The apostles continued to bear powerful witness to the resurrection of the Lord Jesus, and an abundance of grace was at work among them all. [34]There were no needy persons among them. Those who owned properties or houses would sell them, bring the proceeds from the sales, [35]and place them in the care and under the authority of the apostles. Then it was distributed to anyone who was in need.

[36]Joseph, whom the apostles nicknamed Barnabas (that is, "one who encourages"), was a Levite from Cyprus. [37]He owned a field, sold it, brought the money, and placed it in the care and under the authority of the apostles.

ONE CHALLENGE

This week, put into practice what you have learned. Identify someone who is "on the outside looking in"—who hasn't said yes to the saving love of God. When you come back together, you can share the names with one another, write them down somewhere, and discuss how you can "share the good news" with them. Of course, this doesn't have to mean drawing a picture on a napkin, or handing them a pamphlet—there plenty of other ways, and perhaps even more effective ways to share the gospel. But one of the things we have to wrestle with personally is that if we aren't eager to share what we have in Jesus . . . have we forgotten how good the good news is?

DEVOTIONAL

The church isn't to be just any sort of community; it is to be the truest sense of community. All other forms of community tap into our fundamental and innate desires for connection and camaraderie, but they are all just shadows of the true reality that is found in Christ. For the early church, their purpose was clear. They all knew why they were there and what they were about. They existed to bear witness to the Resurrection and participate in the rule and reign of God. This is where their life as individuals was found and what their shared life together was about.

Day 1

Read Matthew 18:10-20

What does this passage have to say about pushing one another forward? Why is it significant that Jesus says, "If your brother or sister sins . . ." instead of "When your brother or sister sins . . ."?

Day 2

Read Proverbs 12:1-28

What wisdom can we glean from these proverbs about challenging one another? How open are you to correction?

Day 3

Read Romans 15:1-33

What does it mean to be patient with others' weakness? In your mind, what is the link between endurance and encouragement? What does it mean for you to have an attitude similar to Christ Jesus' attitude? How does this passage encourage or challenge you?

Day 4

Read Proverbs 18:1-24

What does this proverb have to say about the danger of gossip? How does this relate to Jesus' teaching in Matthew 18:15-20?

Day 5

Read 1 Thessalonians 4:1-18

It seems the author is encouraged by the church's love for one another, but what does he mean in verse 10 when he says to love one another even more? How do we practically do that? What does that imply about our shared life together?

Day 6

Read Romans 14:1-23

The church in Rome was experiencing a lot of division, mainly around religious beliefs and ethnic issues. According to this passage, what are some of the underlying issues driving these conflicts? What does this passage have to say about our shared life together? Who do you tend to pass judgment on? How does this passage challenge you?

Day 7

Read 1 Corinthians 12:1-31

What does this chapter say about the benefits of our shared life together? How do unity and diversity go hand in hand in the life of the church? How do you, or how can you, use your gifts and abilities to help the church carry out its function as the body of Christ?

Session 5:

PUSHING ONE ANOTHER FORWARD

As a group, you have been equipped with all of the tools you need through the first four weeks of the ONE experience. So there's much less reading for this week. Now it's time to roll up our sleeves and get to work; our main focus will be on the group experience, and how you will craft your covenant statement and determine your ground rules for the group. This time will only be valuable to the extent that you invest in it. Decide now to offer your best effort to benefit the growth of the group.

THE THREE QUESTIONS

By now you have more than likely gotten more comfortable with these questions. For the last several weeks we've focused on a specific question. This week, answer whichever question jumps out at you. But you should also feel free to allow everyone to answer all three if you choose to do so.

1. What are you grateful for?

2. What are you anxious about?

3. What are you learning?

MISSION STATEMENTS

Every good company has a defining mission statement that makes clear what they are about. Take a look at the following mission statements and see if you can identify which company they belong to:

1. "To be one of the world's leading producers and providers of entertainment and information. . . . We seek to develop the most creative, innovative and profitable entertainment experiences and related products in the world."

a. Gerber
b. Walt Disney
c. Pixar

2. "To be Earth's most customer-centric company; to build a place where people can come to find and discover anything they might want to buy online."

a. Zappos
b. Amazon
c. Frito-Lay

3. "To give people the power to share and make the world more open and connected."

a. Facebook
b. AT&T
c. ADT Home Security

4. "To bring inspiration and innovation to every athlete in the world."

a. Dunkin' Donuts
b. Icy Hot
c. Nike

Dunkin' Donuts brings inspiration and innovation to every athlete in the world. You have to admit that's pretty funny. Here are the answers: 1.b; 2.b; 3.a; 4.c. How did you do? There were a couple of tricky ones in there, but you likely didn't have a hard time matching each company with its mission statement. Why is that? It's because these companies have taken their mission statements seriously, and it is apparent in the products they make.

That's what a good mission statement does. It provides guidelines for what the organization will or will not do, how its members will and will not function. These statements describe the mission and goal of each organization and help employees know what larger purpose they serve.

That's essentially what your covenant statement will do for your small group. Over the next three weeks, you will zero in on each of the three Core Practices, and the group will decide what these are going to look like and how they will practically be carried out in your group. You will then use all of that information to write your own group's covenant statement.

The focus for this session is on the first Core Practice, pushing one another forward. Lets start to wrestle with what this practice is going to look like in your group.

Spend some time individually answering the prompts at the top of the next three pages. Spend around ten minutes thinking through this individually, and then share together as a group.

What words, phrases, or pictures come to mind when you think about the practice of pushing one another forward? See pages 48–49 in Chapter 2 if you need a refresher on pushing one another forward. Draw or write as many things as you can, even if they seem far-fetched or strange.

How you have experienced being pushed forward in a negative way? How have you seen this practice do damage or cause hurt, whether to you or to someone else?

How have you have experienced being pushed forward in a positive way? How have you seen this practice help heal and transform someone?

How are you going to do it?

So now that you have a sense of what it means to push one another forward, how are you going to do it? Remember that this is a practice and not just a concept, which means it must spill over into your regular interactions with one another. For example, you may make it a point to answer the three questions we have been asking of one another each week, or you may develop your own accountability questions. Or you could begin by sharing what areas of your life you need some pushing forward in, and make it a point to check in with one another every week. Spend some time brainstorming ways to carry out this practice with one another, and write that into your covenant statement as well. Take some notes on your group's discussion in the space below.

Group Discussion: How will your group push one another forward?

If your group is able to come a to a consensus on the practice of pushing one another, then write it down in space provided for your group's covenant statement on the next-to-last page of this journal. You may also choose to write it down on a large piece of paper, markerboard, or chalkboard in your meeting space, so that you can display it next week. Then give each other a high-five. If not, don't worry, you can still give each other a high-five, and at the same time you can revisit it later and continue to work through it until you feel like you are all clear on how you are going to push each other forward.

DEVOTIONAL

We are these walking, talking dichotomies. We long for community and connection, but we are broken versions of ourselves and so we hide from one of the things we have been wired for—each other. No wonder one of the first signs that God's redemptive plan had taken a giant leap forward was this beautiful demonstration of community: Former strangers from all over the world opened up their homes and ate together with glad and sincere hearts. The gospel challenges us to a deeper level of intimacy with one another than what most of us are used to. This will not always be easy and it is guaranteed to be uncomfortable at times, but I can promise you that it will be worth it. Life is an incredible gift, and like most gifts, it is better when it is shared.

Day 1

Read Matthew 7:1-14

In addition to prayer and our dependence on God, what do these verses also say about our commitment to one another? What does this say about how God prefers to work in our lives?

Day 2

Read Galatians 6:1-10

What does this passage have to say about our commitment to one another? What does it mean to bear one another's burdens? How is that countercultural to the day and age in which we live?

Day 3

Read Matthew 7:1-5

Often, what bothers us the most in other people is what bothers us the most about ourselves. How does this passage demonstrate that reality? How can our awareness of this impact our relationships for the better?

Day 4

Read James 2:12-19

What does this passage have to say about what our relationships should look like? Recall a time when you provided for someone in this way or they provided for you. How did that impact your feeling of closeness with God? Explain.

Day 5

Read 1 Thessalonians 5:1-28

This passage was written to a community that was going through fierce persecution. What does it have to say about how we are to be there for one another? What does it mean to encourage one another?

Day 6

Read Psalm 26

One of the great enemies to experiencing a deeper connection with one another is duplicity—pretending to be someone we aren't. What insights does this psalm offer us about dealing with our tendency towards duplicity? Pray your way through the psalm in light of the various ways you struggle to take hold of the undivided life Jesus offers us.

Day 7

Read 1 John 4:7-21

What is your favorite part of this passage? Why? How should our knowledge and experience of God's love for us influence the way we love one another? How does this make loving others more challenging? How does it improve our love for one another?

Session 6:

LIFTING ONE ANOTHER UP

Y ou group is well on its way to laying a foundation that will allow for real, genuine community. You have agreed to be a community with one life, one mind, one heart, and one way. Last week, you discussed the practice of pushing one another forward and how that will take shape in your group. This week, you will focus on the practice of lifting one another up. Again, what you get out of this is all about how you approach it. Commit once again to putting in the hard work to foster community in your group.

THE THREE QUESTIONS

Before you begin, catch up with one another by answering the three questions.

1. What are you grateful for?

2. What are you anxious about?

3. What are you learning?

THE IMPORTANCE OF TRUST

The practice of lifting one another up depends a lot on the amount of trust in the group. Trust is the foundation of vulnerability. When people trust others they are able to be their true selves. Trust gives permission for compassion. When there is trust in a relationship, individuals sense the right to feel what others are feeling and to help in time of need. Trust facilitates grace. Through mutual trust, people can truly extend grace as they are vulnerable with one another and compassionate toward one another.

Hopefully, in the last session you were able to name how your group will push one another forward. This week, you will decide how the group will practice lifting one another up.

Once again, spend at least ten minutes working through this individually using the prompts on the following pages, and then share with one another.

What words, phrases, or pictures come to mind when you think about the practice of lifting one another up? Reread pages 49–50 of Chapter 2 if you need a refresher on lifting each other up. There are no wrong answers; just write whatever comes to mind and pay attention to what really jumps out at you.

How have you have experienced being lifted up, or lifting someone else up, in a negative way? How have you seen this practice do damage or cause hurt?

How have you experienced being lifted up, or lifting someone else up, in a positive way? How have you seen this practice help heal and transform people?

How are you going to do it?

After sharing with one another, spend some time brainstorming how you can practically implement it in your group. Maybe you have a phone tree in case an emergency happens, or you each share a list of things you need done at your home, or you start by identifying one another's gifts, talents, and assets. . . . I mean knowing who has a pickup truck would be a really good thing, am I right? Spend the rest of your time together deciding how you will lift each other up in practical, real ways. Then think about how best to express this in your covenant statement. Take some notes on your group's discussion in the space below.

Group Discussion: How will your group lift one another up?

If your group is able to come a to a consensus on the practice of lifting one another up, write it alongside your commitment to pushing one another forward in the space provided for your group's covenant statement on the next-to-last page of this journal. Add it to your display as well, so that your group can see how the full covenant statement is coming together. Once again you can continue this conversation if need be down the road, but recognize the gift that this conversation has been. It's good to know that you have a group of people in your corner!

DEVOTIONAL

Not only was the early church of one mind and one heart, they were committed to heading one way: outward. You see, the kingdom of God is an inside-out kingdom; it is outwardly oriented. It's in the Kingdom's nature to grow, to expand, and to welcome in those who are currently on the outside. The gospel is the kind of news that can't keep quiet or stay to itself. It has been changing people's lives and flipping the world right-side up for over two thousand years, and it's not done yet.

Day 1

Read Luke 13:10-17

How does the woman's encounter with Jesus differ from the religious leader's encounter with Jesus? What does this passage have to teach us about the inside-out nature of the kingdom of God?

Day 2

Read Luke 18:9-14

What is the point of the parable about the Pharisee and tax collector? How does this speak to the inside-out nature of the kingdom of God?

Day 3

Read Isaiah 19:19-25

What is significant about there being an altar in the heart of Egypt? What does this passage have to say about the nature of God?

Day 4

Read John 4:1-42

The kingdom of God doesn't pay attention to the labels and categories in which we often we place one another. How does this encounter speak to that? Have you ever felt labeled or categorized? How did it feel? Who do you tend to label?

Day 5

Read Psalm 145

What does this psalm have to say to us about community? Who poured into you and led you to place your trust in God?

Day 6

Read Colossians 3:1-25

This chapter is all about living out the reality of our salvation (being hidden with Christ). How much of Paul's instruction has to do with our shared life together? What does this mean about the importance of community in the life of a Jesus follower?

Day 7

Read Luke 5:17-26

What do you admire about the men who lowered their friend to Jesus? What motivated them to do such a thing? Who would you be willing to do that for? Who is someone that you want to see put their faith in Jesus? Commit to praying for them every day for the next six weeks.

Session 7:

SENDING
ONE ANOTHER OUT

I f you are going to truly follow the lead of the early church and be the kind of community that enjoys the goodwill or respect of all the people (see Acts 2:47), then you will have to determine how your group will send one another out. A small group who has truly centered itself on the gospel will be one whose existence is somehow impacting the world around it.

THE THREE QUESTIONS

Before you begin to work through this, spend some time catching up by answering the three questions below.

1. What are you grateful for?

2. What are you anxious about?

3. What are you learning?

It is now time to continue shaping your group's covenant statement. In the last two weeks, you should have decided on the portions of your covenant statement that have to do with pushing one another forward and lifting one another up. This week you will decide how the group will send one another out. As in previous weeks, this session will only be as valuable as the effort each member puts forth. It is important for each group member to speak up and for each group member to be heard.

Spend some time, about ten minutes, working through the following exercises individually and then share with one another.

What words, phrases, or pictures come to mind when you think about the practice of sending one another out? Perhaps you think of making a difference, meeting a need, or reaching out to those who are on the outside looking in. Reread pages 50–52 of Chapter 2 if you need a refresher on sending one another out. Write or draw as much as you can, whatever comes to mind.

How have you experienced the practice of sending one another out in a negative way? Has someone sent you out, or have you sent someone else out, in a way that caused harm?

How have you experienced the practice of sending one another out in a positive way? Has someone sent you out, or have you sent someone else out, in a way that led to transformation and positive change?

How are you going to do it?

Once you have shared your individual responses with one another, spend some time discussing practical ways this practice can become a part of your shared life. Here are a few other questions you may find helpful:

What in your community breaks your heart or makes you angry? Often our calling comes from a place of disruption—when we become aware of what is not "OK" in the world around us.

What do you love to do more than anything? What are the unique skills, abilities, and resources present in your group that could be an asset to God's kingdom?

Frederick Buechner once said, "The place God calls you to is the place where your deep gladness and the world's deep hunger meet." (From *Wishful Thinking: A Theological ABC*; Harper and Row, 1973; page 95). Discuss how your answers to the above questions could be pointing your group to a calling from God. Take some notes on your group's discussion in the space below.

Group Discussion: How will you send one another out?

If you are able to agree on what sending one another out is going to look like in your group, add it to your commitment to push each other forward and lift each other up on the next-to-last page of this journal. Add it to your markerboard, chalkboard, or paper display as well, so that you can see your full covenant statement. If necessary, spend some time refining the language of your covenant statement until you all agree upon it. This covenant statement will be your defining expression of mission and purpose, so it's well worth the time!

It's important to discuss how you can ensure that this covenant statement becomes the unifying purpose that empowers you to stay of one mind. Perhaps everyone in the group could carry around a card with it written down, or you perhaps you could continue displaying it in the room whenever you meet. You may also wish to recite it together periodically when you meet. The goal is that your covenant statement doesn't just get lost in the pages of this book, but that it really does become the heartbeat for your shared life together.

DEVOTIONAL

There is a depth to our life with God that we can only experience when we come together—when we are one. When we find ourselves asking, "Where is God?" perhaps a better question for us to ask is "Where are we?" Where are we in regards to our commitment to one another? When we cut ourselves off from community, we simultaneously separate ourselves from one of the primary ways in which God prefers to work in our lives. The most important thing for us to know right now as we journey toward a shared life is that our involvement with Christ-centered community is not optional. It is absolutely foundational.

Day 1

Read 2:42-47 and Acts 4:32-37

After everything you have learned about these passages, what is now your favorite aspect of how the early believers lived together? What do you think will be the biggest struggle for you and your group to implement together? What can you do about it?

Day 2

Read Genesis 2:1-25

Right from the beginning we see that human beings were wired for relationship. How does this chapter describe that aspect of what it means to be human? What does it mean that they were naked and felt no shame? Do you have any relationships in your life that have that quality? Explain.

Day 3

Read Genesis 3:1-24

In Genesis 2, we saw that God created human beings for deep, intimate relationships with one another. Genesis 3 is when sin enters the picture and messes all it up. What do you notice from Genesis 3 about how sin impacts us relationally? What does this look like in your life today?

Read Genesis 11:1-9 and Acts 2:1-13

How is what happens in Acts 2 a reversal of what had happened in Genesis 11? What does this mean about what God is doing through Jesus Christ and the church? What does this mean about our personal commitment to community?

Day 5

Read 1 Thessalonians 3:1-13

What does this chapter have to say about our shared life together? How does the example of our faith encourage one another? Who do you have in your life who lifts you up like this? Take some time today and let them know how much that means to you.

Day 6

Read Ephesians 3:14–4:16

According to this passage, is it possible to experience the full height, width, and depth of God apart from our shared life together? Why or why not? How have you yourself experienced the vastness of God's love through community? How does this passage encourage you?

Day 7

Read Matthew 18:15-20

Jesus says that when two or three are gathered together in his name, he is there with them. How have you experienced the presence of Jesus so far in your time with the group?

Session 8:

GROUND RULES AND LIFE STORIES

This is the last session before you are on your own. How about that? In this session, you and your group will work to develop some ground rules that will shape how you will spend your time together. But first, spend a few minutes sharing what has been going on in your lives over the past week.

THE THREE QUESTIONS

Take some time for each of you to answer the three questions.

1. What are you grateful for?

2. What are you anxious about?

3. What are you learning?

The Ground Rules

Your covenant statement captures what your group will do with one another, whereas the ground rules are focused on how you will do that. In order to prepare yourself for this important discussion, each of you, on your own, spend a few minutes finishing the drawing below.

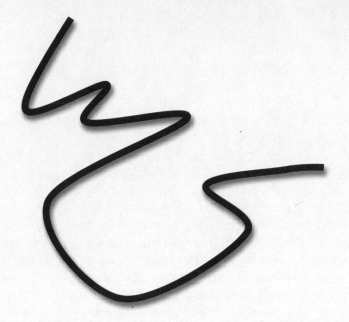

I'm sure you discovered that everyone's finished drawing didn't turn out the same way. For one, the instructions were really vague. There were no specifics given in terms of what the drawing should be; it was left open for interpretation. This speaks to the importance of our covenant statements. The covenant statement informs us about what sort of picture we are trying to draw, so to speak. It provides a guide about our common goal, our purpose in gathering and sharing life together. As followers of Jesus, our shared life isn't just centered around any purpose, but the purpose—the gospel of the kingdom of God.

At the same time, we all look at that curvy line from different perspectives and as a result we see the potential for different finished pictures. Essentially, we aren't all coming to it from the same place. The truth is, how your day has been going thus far may somehow influence the picture you have drawn.

This helps to explain the importance of the group's ground rules. Our individual, personal rules are the perspectives through which we understand the world. We all have different rules, which can be anything from personal guidelines to preferred working styles to even pet peeves. This becomes readily apparent when two people get married. For one person, a rule is that shoes belong wherever you happen to take them off when you get home, but the other person's rule is that shoes belong in the closet. You can see where operating according to different rules can open the door for a whole lot of conflict.

Ground rules establish some common understanding, an agreed-upon starting point for navigating your shared life together. Personal rules will always differ, but if everyone adheres to the common ground rules, conflict will be minimized and your relationships will benefit from everyone being on the same page. As you work through your individual reflections and group discussion, keep in mind the three Core Postures of vulnerability, compassion, and grace. Your group's ground rules should reflect these Core Postures and assist you in living them out among your group.

In order to establish some rules of your own, begin by identifying potential barriers or roadblocks that could keep the group from being as healthy as possible. Spend the next ten minutes reflecting individually on the questions below in the space provided. Then discuss your answers as a group.

Write or draw some of your own personal rules that you live by and, consciously or not, expect others to live by.

Write or draw potential conflicts that can arise in your group when two or more people have different unspoken rules. These can be hypothetical situations or actual experiences that you have had or witnessed. Come up with as many as you can.

Write or draw your own ideas for agreed-upon ground rules that can help minimize group conflict.

How are you going to do it?

Once you've spent time reflecting as individuals, share your ideas and thoughts with one another about what ground rules should shape your life together.

This conversation is so valuable. For instance, let's consider the issue of "the dominator"—you know, a person in a group who tends to take over the conversation most weeks. This is, of course, one of the more awkward issues for the group to deal with. How exactly do you tell someone they are talking too much? The truth is, the biggest reason why it is so awkward is because we don't talk about it until it's a problem. However, imagine a group that has had this conversation beforehand and has agreed upon a common way for dealing with it. As an example, I know of groups who have code words that they use when someone is controlling the conversation. The code words help to keep things lighthearted, gently drawing someone's attention to the fact that it's someone else's turn to speak. Of course, there are times when it is obvious that someone's issue needs to be front and center at a group gathering. As a group, you will eventually be able to discern when focused attention on one person is needed and when it is just a bad habit. A ground rule involving an issue like this helps to inform the group on how they should respond and at the same time makes it really hard for the dominator to be offended when the ground rule is invoked. After all, they were part of establishing the ground rule.

Establishing and tweaking your ground rules will be an ongoing practice as you seek to share life together out of the three Core Postures. This is a learn-as-you-go sort of thing, but commit now to be the kind of group that is committed to working through conflict in order to grow closer together. Take some notes on your group's discussion in the space below.

Group Discussion: What are some ground rules you could put in place that will reflect the three Core Postures of vulnerability, compassion, and grace?

Be sure to write your group's ground rules down so that you can all remember them. Space is provided on the last page of this journal for ground rules. You should also display them alongside your covenant statement, and remind yourselves of these ground rules periodically. It may be a good idea for your group leader to quickly outline the ground rules at the beginning of every meeting, though some groups may find that this is unnecessary. The important thing is that all group members agree to follow the ground rules, making them a practical step toward embodying vulnerability, compassion, and grace in your life together.

WHERE TO GO FROM HERE . . .

We're now at the end of our eight-week ONE Curriculum. So what happens next week? Here are some guidelines for continuing to meet as you deepen your relationships, push each other forward, lift each other up, and send each other out.

Continue the Three Questions

Keep checking in with one another at the beginning of every meeting using the Three Questions: What are you grateful for? What are you anxious about? What are you learning? These may seem repetitive after a while, but eventually you'll find deeper meaning to your conversations, as well as new occasions for vulnerability, compassion, and grace to develop. They will help your group establish a rhythm and give you all some common vocabulary for talking about your spiritual lives.

Continue the Conversation

Don't feel like you have to complete your group's covenant statement or ground rules by the end of the eighth week. It's great if you can do that, but many groups will need longer. Don't rush it. The covenant statement and the ground rules are both vital to the group's life together, so it's worth taking extra time and hard work together to get them right. Continue the conversation for as long as necessary. Perhaps you will need to set a few minutes aside each week until you feel like you have them established.

Share Your Stories

This will be your next big task as a group. Once your group is meeting on your own, you will deepen your relationships with one another by sharing and interacting with one another's life stories. This is a practical exercise of compassion and vulnerability—taking some time to walk in someone else's shoes, and at the same time allowing them to walk around in yours.

When it comes to sharing our stories, there are typically two types of people. First, for some of us there is an obvious moment in our past when we first said yes to the saving love of God, a time when it felt like Jesus changed everything. If this is you, then a simple way to share your story would be by answering the following questions:

> Who were you before you met Jesus?
> How did you meet Jesus?
> What is your life with Jesus like right now?
> Where do you want Jesus to take you from here?

Second, there are some of us who have a really hard time identifying one moment that changed everything. Perhaps we can't remember a time when Jesus wasn't a part of our lives; there is no dramatic conversion experience, just a steady relationship. That's OK. We all have an important story to tell. If this is you, you may find it helpful to identify several of the most significant moments in your life that have shaped who you are. These can be good or bad; what's important is that they played a significant role in your life and faith. What are some of the biggest life transitions you have experienced? How did you navigate them, and how did they impact you? There really is no wrong way to do this. The important thing is to give people some sort of understanding of who you are and where you come from.

Remember, you do not have to share your deepest, darkest secrets right away. Start with what you are comfortable sharing, and be committed to opening up more and more when the time is right.

Its important for us to listen actively to one another's stories as well. In order to encourage this, everyone will be asked to make a comment and ask a question. What is something you appreciated about their story, and what would you like to hear more about? Of course the same question doesn't need to be asked more than once, and the person sharing his or her story doesn't have to answer a question if he or she isn't ready to do so.

Before you leave, schedule out who is going to share and when. This way, each person has time to prepare to share his or her story. Do not schedule more than two stories per gathering to ensure that you have plenty of time to interact with one another, to truly listen, and to appreciate what each person has to say. You will likely find that only one person should share each week.

Throw a Party

Once you have your covenant statement and ground rules, and after you have engaged with one another's stories, it's time to party. The Book of Acts tells us that the early church ate together with glad and sincere hearts. Bottom line: They knew how to have a good time together. You can go out to dinner, gather in someone's home for a potluck or meal, or have a picnic at a local park. Your group will know best what options are available and meet everyone's needs and desires. Whatever you do, just make sure there is good food involved, a lot of laughing, and a time of naming and celebrating what God has done in your midst. The people of God should throw the best parties.

Keep Going

After eight weeks together, you have everything you need to get your shared life started off on the right foot. Your covenant statement lays out what you will do together, and your ground rules help to inform how you will do that. My hope is that you and your group are excited and expectant for God to move in your midst.

Even though you are finished with ONE, in reality you are just getting started. I can promise you, this will not be easy; it may be one of the hardest things you have ever done, and it will certainly require you to fight for it. But it is and always will be worth it.

If you have made it this far, then that means you "get it." You sense why this matters and what a greater commitment to our shared life in Christ can and will do in you. For me, there is an itch that once-a-week church just can't scratch. There's a longing for something more. Chances are you know what I mean, because you have that itch as well.

Jesus' vision for his church goes way beyond a once-a-week gathering with virtual strangers. His hope and expectation is that those of us who have said yes to the saving love of God would move closer and closer to one another. His hope is that in each other, we would have people to do life with, fighting shoulder to shoulder for one another's marriages, helping to raise one another's children, working to bring justice to the poor and oppressed, laughing together, crying together, and eating together. I think in all of us there is a desire for the world to be different, to be better, to look more like the place we know that it was meant to be. That's the role of the church—to show people what the life of God looks like and to bring God's promised future into the present by how we live…TOGETHER as ONE.

So may we in Christ's church move closer to one another.

May we have the courage to open ourselves up, to see and to be seen.

May we who are many become one.

COVENANT STATEMENT

GROUND RULES